Here's What People Are Saying About

THE ULTIMATE GUIDE FOR THE AVID INDOORSMAN

"This book is very important."

INTERNATIONAL SOCIETY OF IMPORTANT THINGS

"Come again? You want me to endorse what?"

BEAR GRYLLS

"You are very special to me!
Please leave a message after the tone."

OPRAH WINFREY…'S VOICE MAIL

"I wish I would have had such a book when I was alive."

WINSTON CHURCHILL

"Finally! This is what we've all been waiting for!"

BRENÉ BROWN (overheard as she reached
the front of the popcorn line at the theater)

"This book is utterly ridiculous[ly well written]."
(emphasis mine)

UNNAMED PUBLISHING EXECUTIVE

"I've read a lot of books."

RICHARD HEDGMONTON,
World Record Holder for Most Books Read

The
ULTIMATE GUIDE
for the AVID
INDOORSMAN

JOHN DRIVER

HARVEST HOUSE PUBLISHERS
EUGENE, OREGON

Cover by Bryce Williamson

Cover image and interior illustrations © by Jordan Highimage

Back cover author photo © by Jeffrey Holland

Published in association with the literary agency of Wolgemuth & Associates, Inc.

The Ultimate Guide for the Avid Indoorsman
Copyright © 2019 by John Driver
Published by Harvest House Publishers
Eugene, Oregon 97408
www.harvesthousepublishers.com

ISBN 978-0-7369-7526-1 (pbk.)
ISBN 978-0-7369-7527-8 (eBook)

Library of Congress Cataloging-in-Publication Data

Names: Driver, John, author.
Title: The ultimate guide for the avid indoorsman : life is better in here /
  John Driver.
Description: Eugene, Oregon : Harvest House Publishers, 2019.
Identifiers: LCCN 2018026626 (print) | LCCN 2018038311 (ebook) | ISBN
  9780736975278 (ebook) | ISBN 9780736975261 (paperback)
Subjects: LCSH: Conduct of life--Humor. | American wit and humor. | BISAC:
  RELIGION / Christian Life / Men's Issues.
Classification: LCC PN6231.C6142 (ebook) | LCC PN6231.C6142 D77 2019 (print)
  | DDC 818/.602--dc23
LC record available at https://lccn.loc.gov/2018026626

Printed in the United States of America

18 19 20 21 22 23 24 25 26 / VP-SK / 10 9 8 7 6 5 4 3 2 1

For Dad,
who cheered me on in every endeavor in life...
and savored my silly writings.

CONTENTS

Introduction: Facing the Great Indoors 13

1. Foundational Elements of Indoorsmanship 17

   1. Defining the Indoors 18

   2. Earliest Origins 18

   3. Practical Definitions and Applications 19

   4. A Brief History of the Indoors 19

      From Caveman to Man Cave

   5. Defining the Antithesis—The Outdoors 24

      Common Expressions Casting the Outdoors in a Positive Light…
      Common Expressions Casting the Outdoors in a Realistic Light…
      Other Common Terms Expressing the Difficulty of the Outdoors

2. Evaluating Your Level of Indoorsmanship 29

   1. Begin at the Beginning 30

   2. The Indooreagram 30

      Twenty Key Questions to Determine Your Level of Indoorsmanship

   3. Grading Your Indooreagram 38

   4. Understanding Your Indooreagram Score 39

      What If I Don't Want to Change? (A History Lesson)… What
      Does My Indooreagram Score Mean?

      Level 1: Avid Outdoorsman

      Level 2: Social Outdoorsman

      Level 3: Casual Indoorsman

      Level 4: Moderate Indoorsman

      Level 5: Avid Indoorsman

3. The Indoorsman vs. the Outdoorsman 59

   1. Diverse Perspectives 59

   2. The Defining Light of Language 60

   3. Indoorsman vs. Outdoorsman Interpretations of
      Common Expressions 61

       *Troubleshooting (vs. Trouble Shooting)…Being Left to His Own
       Devices…A Slippery Slope…Outstanding in His Field (vs.
       Out Standing in His Field)…Cliffhanger…Breaching a Firewall
       (vs. Breaching a Fire Wall)…Hacking…Don't Poke the Bear…
       Stable Employment*

4. The Greatest Dangers of the Great Indoors 75

   1. Differing Philosophies and Common Fears 75

   2. FOMA (Fear of Miscellaneous Assembly) 76

       *Kitchen Appliances…Bathroom Fixtures…Indoor Furniture…
       Miscellaneous Deck and Pool Paraphernalia…Children's Toys
       Assembled on Christmas Eve…Children's Toys Assembled on
       Christmas Day*

   3. The Indoor Fear of Repair 84

       Repair Problem 1: Plumbing…Repair Problem 2: Doors

5. The Greatest Dangers of the Outdoors 97

   1. General Creeping and Crawling Things 97

       Snakes

   2. All Creatures Bigfoot and Small…and Bigger 99

       Bigfoot…Loch Ness Monster

   3. Dirt 103

   4. Water Dangers 105

       Rivers…Oceans

   5. Unpredictable Weather 107

   6. The Sun and Sunburns 107

   7. Quicksand 111

6. Establishing a Healthy Indoors Routine 113

   1. The Healthy Routine of Sleep 114

     Hours of Sleep…Most Common Sleep Deterrents…
     Choosing a Mattress

   2. The Healthy Routine of Exercise 119

     Philosophy…Standing Up Occasionally…Finger Circuit
     Training…Other Miscellaneous Exercises and the Modem Plank

   3. The Healthy Routine of Eating 122

     Perceptions and Realities…Portion Control…Domestic Indoor
     Radiation (Microwave)…Indoorsman Nutritional Thought…
     The Indoorsman Dietary Cycle at Work…The Art of Snacking

   4. The Healthy Routine of Drinking Coffee 137

     A Semi-Brief Brief on the History of Coffee…Brewing
     Techniques… Quantity Control vs. Quality Control

7. How to Dress and Act Like an Avid Indoorsman 143

   1. Simple 143

   2. Sleek 145

   3. Sweatpants 147

   4. Honorable Mentionables: Slippers 151

   5. Indoorsman Situational Clothing Ethics 155

     Office Appropriate

   6. The Indoorsman's Hygiene 157

     Philosophy…Showering…Beard Care

8. The Indoorsman's Guide to Miscellaneous Situations 171

   1. Ergonomic Convenience 171

     Couch…Recliner

2. Transportation 177

*Automobiles…Indoorsman Automobile Recommendations…
Other Forms of Ground Transportation*

3. Pet Ownership 182

*Three Determining Factors for Choosing and Managing Indoor
Pets…Five Most Recommended Pets for the Indoorsman*

4. Sports 185

Sports-Resistant Indoorsmen…Sports-Interested Indoorsmen

5. Tattoos 187

6. Hobbies 189

*Wikipedia Editor…Yoga…3D Printing…Crossword Puzzles…
Fantasy Sports…Learning a Foreign Language…Genealogy…
Other Possible Indoorsman Hobbies*

7. Other Miscellaneous Situations 193

*Three Secrets for Moving Quietly Through a House in the Dark…
Loss of Wi-Fi…Toilet Paper Outage*

9. Connecting with People Indoors 197

1. Your Spouse 197

*Designate Bathrooms…Make Yours a Double…Do Not Watch
Ahead*

2. Your Kids 198

*Install Master Bedroom Locks…When They Won't Answer, Just
Leave the Bathroom Door Unlocked*

3. Your Dog 200

*Invest in a Doggie Bed…Develop an Alter Ego and Accompanying
Voice for Your Dog…Blame Your Dog for Outrageous Things*

4. Your Family and Friends 201

Set More Than a Starting Time…Buy a Floor-Cleaning Robot

5. Connecting in Public Indoor Spaces 203
    Beware the Meet and Greet...Seek Out Indoorsman
    Ways to Engage...Master a Few Elements of Small Talk
6. Connecting with the Outdoorsman Using Acceptable Gibberish . . 205
7. Other Miscellaneous Connection Issues 206
    Fist Bumping...Call Screening...When You Must Go Outdoors

Conclusion: Putting It All Together 213

FACING THE GREAT INDOORS

There he stood, heart pounding in his chest like some deranged jackhammer. Sweat beading upon the ever-increasing hairless surface of his brow.

And yet he'd never felt more alive.

His adversary was relentless, but he stood his ground. With every decisive jolt of his arms, the battle grew even fiercer. Give. Take. Dart. Retreat. But he would not—no, he *could not* lose. He was made for this moment.

And then it happened. With one final, desperate flailing of his wrist, warm liquid suddenly cascaded upon his dirty hands from the freshly opened orifice of his enemy—and he felt the sweet victory flowing fast and free between his fingers. It was a cleansing.

You are no doubt asking, "What sort of ferocious wild animal had he slain with his bare hands?"

A great question. But actually this particular brush with danger occurred in the dimly lit and not-so-recently-serviced restroom of his local movie theater. His nemesis? It was none other than one of those motion-sensor faucets...the nefarious ones that are up to no good. No matter how much one waves his fingers in front of the sensor, these beastly contraptions simply refuse to acknowledge the existence of one's hands.

Well, not *his* hands (long, dramatic pause)...not *this* time.

Sure, he may have looked like a complete idiot waving wildly in front of the sink in the men's restroom. Sure, he may have freaked out the two little boys standing next to him who, incidentally, seemed to be having no trouble whatsoever with their faucet…which didn't stop them at all from crying when he started to drop-kick the soap dispenser. Sure, the theater management may have asked him to leave.

Sure, all of this may be true, but the question must be asked: Did the indoors conquer him? The answer is…well, mostly it did not. (The water only flowed for about three seconds before his hands apparently became invisible again…hence, the "mostly" part.)

Tomato, tomahto.

Regardless, the results of experiences such as these are the manifesto you hold in your very visible hands. This book is a clarion call to all Avid Indoorsmen of the world—and yes, even to those who haven't yet dreamed they could become such because they don't yet possess the emotional fortitude, the elite skill set, or the cool T-shirt being presently designed that will set them apart for the task. Regardless, when you put this book back into the magazine basket in your bathroom, you will finally be fully equipped to survive this and even more epic indoor dangers…or you will have a new, overpriced, rectangular coaster for your coffee table.

Either way, something, though perhaps nonspecific, will have definitely happened.

No matter what the more socially accepted colloquialism may insist, the truth is that it's as much a jungle *in* there as it is *out* there. For far too long, a global tribe of brave Indoorsmen have needlessly languished in the shadows of shame and obscurity…or in some cases, just their parents' basements. No more! It is time to rise… unless you're presently sitting in a massage chair that has your arms and legs comfortably restrained. In that case, go ahead and finish your massage…and *then* rise!

It's okay. The global tribe will wait for you.

You may find it surprising that many Indoorsmen have actually spent much of their lives in the great outdoors. Contrary to popular belief, the great Indoorsmen of the world are not necessarily anti-Outdoorsmen. They may be hunters, fishermen, runners, golfers. In other words, they may have conquered the outdoors. So if you think you have to forsake the outdoors altogether to be an Avid Indoorsman, nothing could be further from the truth.

However, the sad reality is that many people who can navigate their way through the wilderness using nothing but the stars, a discarded snakeskin, and the faint scent of badger urine (that is probably how it works) can still somehow become utterly lost when they simply cross the threshold into their own indoor spaces. You probably know someone like this in your own life. You'll probably want to conceal his identity, but he may or may not be the father of your wife or husband. (And you may or may not get a Christmas present this year.)

This nameless man is a rugged Outdoorsman. If it crawls, swims, walks, or flies, he's shot it, stuffed it, and hung it on his mantel. He is a man's man. Perhaps you once watched in awe as he ate an entire bowl of cedar bark in one sitting…just because he could.

Or maybe those were pretzels.

At any rate, the disturbing dichotomy is that you have probably also witnessed this expert Outdoorsman fall to his knees, weeping openly with the loud cries of a schoolgirl scorned because, after hours of failed attempts, he still could not identify the correct input button on his remote control. You have probably sat with him in front of a top-of-the-line, 75-inch, ultra-high-definition television, only to find yourself watching the football game on a 30-inch standard-def image displayed in the middle of this pristine screen…all because he was still using an RCA cable instead of an HDMI cable.

As you recall this moment, perhaps a single tear just stained your page.

Listen, you just can't sit back and watch this anymore…mainly because you can't see his screen unless you move much closer. But also, in a larger metaphorical and abstract sense, you really can't watch it happen anymore. These severe cases of Indoorsmen Deficiency—or ID—must be treated.

In fact, if this book only reaches a single person out there, then…well, the author will probably never sign a book deal again. Not sure about the significance of this, but since the author's backspace button is broken (true story), he's just going to keep writing, and you should probably just keep reading. The point is that someone cares enough to reach out and make a difference in the lives of Indoorsmen everywhere…or at least contribute a few pages to their emergency plan for catastrophic toilet paper outages.

Regarding the term "Indoorsmen," let's not forget the brave Indoors*women* out there as well. Ever heard of Rosie the Riveter? It's not as if she was fabricating bomb casings out in an open field under the stars. She was a master of the indoors—and the reason the Allies won the war and we're not all speaking German today. So everywhere you see the term "he" in this book, feel free to substitute "she" as well. Indoorsmanship is not limited or confined by gender, race, or background. It is for everyone.

Throughout the pages ahead, you will learn to define the differences between the indoors and the outdoors—and the dangers of each, many of which are overlooked by a culture seemingly slanted toward Outdoorsmen. This book will attempt to invert that slant or perhaps determine the proverbial cosign or tangent of its angle. After all, it was Archimedes who said, "Give me a lever long enough and a fulcrum on which to place it, and I'll start the carnival roller coaster… Hey, kid, fasten thy harness!" Or something like that.

You will become equipped not only to survive and thrive in the indoors but also to waste time while you're doing it. After all, any old book could teach you how to build a shelter and survive in the great outdoors, but how many could teach you how to conquer the perils that already exist in the biggest shelter you already own?

The answer is one…exactly one book can do this.

There will be laughing. There will be crying. There will be blood. But enough about opening your kid's juice pouch. This book will be pretty intense as well.

Are you ready to become the Avid Indoorsman you never knew you were dreaming of becoming? If so, feel free to simply allow the residue from the Popsicle you are eating that has stuck the paper to your fingers to cause you to turn the page, albeit however sweetly and inadvertently.

FOUNDATIONAL ELEMENTS OF INDOORSMANSHIP

*The mass of men lead lives of
quiet desperation [indoors].*

HENRY DAVID THOREAU

What is the indoors? How does it differ from the outdoors? How can one anticipate all that life within the unpredictable indoors may throw at them? How do they learn to throw things back?

WINDOWS CLOSED
TO CONTROL
INDOOR CLIMATE

ROOF TO PROTECT
FROM NATURAL
ELEMENTS

4 WALLS TO
MAKE INDOOR
SPACE

DOOR: CRUCIAL
FOR STATUS OF BEING
WITHIN DOORS

1. DEFINING THE INDOORS

IN-DOORS: [in-dawrs, -dohrs] adv. *also IN-DOOR:* singular. adj. 1. In or into a house or building. Occurring, used, etc., in a house or building, rather than out of doors. Aphetic variant of *within-door,* orig. phrase *within (the) door,* i.e., inside the house.

What does it take to achieve at least a pedestrian mastery of Indoorsmanship, much less the rare status of Avid Indoorsman?

The journey to a complete understanding of Indoorsmanship is not for the faint of heart—although those with heart conditions are by no means disqualified from achieving the highest levels of expertise. Regardless of age, gender, intelligence, fitness level, or experience, we must begin by addressing that which appears to be obvious and thus is often overlooked or dismissed. Just as any sound structure is erected upon a solid, well-engineered foundation, those Avid Indoorsmen who may indeed inhabit said structures must also be willing to engage the educational and intellectual processes of laying the right mental, physical, and emotional foundations for this way of life and living. So, then, one must attune his or her ear to the sounds of Indoorsmanship training.

After all, unlike a forest, if a tree falls indoors, everyone hears it.

2. EARLIEST ORIGINS

The first recorded appearance of a variation of the term "indoors" was the word "in-door," which surfaced as early as 1711. By 1750 the concept had undergone a somewhat sophisticated vernacular evolution into the phrase "within doors," but this version did not possess the convenience that brevity affords the popular lexicon. By 1759 the more modern form of the word—"indoors"—was being used with regularity, and by 1801 it had spawned its adjective cousin: "indoor" (i.e., an indoor space).

3. PRACTICAL DEFINITIONS AND APPLICATIONS

The simplest practical definition of the indoors is "the area or space inside a building."

This may sound simple enough, but there are many nuances to defining the indoors in relation to the various climates and terrains that may be encountered therein. To many Novice Indoorsmen, "climate" and "terrain" may sound like foreign concepts to the discipline of Indoorsmanship itself, but such stereotypical and shallow understanding is the very reason so many people suffer the ill effects of inadequate Indoorsmanship. Many of these effects, as well as their antithetical remedies, will be described in meticulous detail throughout the forthcoming content. For now, it suffices to say that Indoorsmanship is an important field of study.[1]

4. A BRIEF HISTORY OF THE INDOORS

The earliest manuscripts of antiquity reveal an instinctive drive among humankind to seek shelter from the climate and elements. At the core of the study of Indoorsmanship is this most basic human desire. While modern interpretations of the Indoorsman color him or her as weak, lazy, or unable to face the difficulties of the outdoors as a result of some general personal character or physical deficiency, history teaches us otherwise. Humankind has always sought the path of Indoorsmanship, for it is embedded in our DNA.

This is why the earliest men and women spent so much of their time seeking better experiences in whatever indoors they were maintaining. From the floor of a cave, amenities arose in the form of round, smooth stones rather than jagged stones to be used for pillows. Even from these primitive beginnings, the location of one's residence became a priority for the Indoorsman, even if this only meant choosing a cave higher up the cliff face that would deter intruders as well as the spray of the rising tides below.

At the root of historical Indoorsmanship was the desire to create an indoor space more apt for survival and thriving than one's predecessors'. This movement

---

1. Not to be confused with actual fields, which are predominantly found only in the outdoors.

from the outdoors to the indoors is still evident in our modern age. Ironically, the best example of this migration is found in the life of the modern Outdoorsman. Though he or she may claim to have a propensity for "roughing it," it is at least odd, if not conclusively telling, that his or her outdoor equipment seeks to make outdoor experiences less and less rough. This is evident in deer stands featuring plush seats almost as comfortable as one's couch, tents so large and luxurious that they boast square footage and property taxes, and RVs that cost more than one's home—bringing all of the comforts of the indoors to the outdoors.

No matter how much the Outdoorsman may protest, this proves that the real goal, even if only subconsciously, is to continually make a better indoor space by making one's outdoor experience more like one's indoor experience.

For argument's sake, try evaluating this subject from a religious perspective. Regardless of one's beliefs or predilection regarding faith, there can be no denial of the biblical directive to pursue Indoorsmanship. The early chapters of Genesis reveal a story in which the Creator sets Adam and Eve in the middle of the most incredible outdoor space imaginable—the Garden of Eden. And yet, even in this paradise, the Creator instructs the young couple to take charge of their surroundings and adapt them to family life. This included gardening, shepherding, and naming the various species they were shepherding.

As they were told to procreate and bring babies into this new world, surely there were expectations that these children would grow and be nourished under whatever family shelter Adam and Eve constructed for them. Yes, it is not out of the question to consider that the divine command to subdue the earth included the construction and subsequent improvement of places upon it in which to live.

A. From Caveman to Man Cave

The list below illustrates the progress of Indoorsmanship throughout history. Please note that this list is not (and indeed could not be) exhaustive because time and space would not permit such a detailed description. For a more comprehensive history of Indoorsmanship, visit your nearest university library, where experts on the subject have produced much more in-depth research.

Stone Age/Early Indoorsmen

- Main Type of Indoor Structure: Caves
- Greatest Fear: Being the human toothpick of a saber-toothed tiger
- Greatest Contribution to Indoorsmanship: A love of dark rooms

Bronze Age Indoorsmen (3300–1200 BC)

- Main Type of Indoor Structure: Rectangular or circular houses constructed from timber beams with thatched roofs made from reeds
- Greatest Fear: Being gored by an "Iron Age pig," a breed that was a cross between a Tamworth and a wild boar
- Greatest Contribution to Indoorsmanship: Indoor plumbing

Iron Age Indoorsmen (1200–550 BC)

- Main Type of Indoor Structure: Round, one-roomed homes with a pointed thatched roof and walls made from wattle and daub (a mixture of mud and twigs)
- Greatest Fear: Being crushed by falling anvils
- Greatest Contribution to Indoorsmanship: Iron skillets (for cooking bacon)

Ancient Mesopotamia/Egypt (3300–30 BC)

- Main Type of Indoor Structure: Mud-brick homes
- Greatest Fear: Sleepwalking off a pyramid in the middle of the night
- Greatest Contribution to Indoorsmanship: Rudimentary forms of text messaging
  (cuneiform, hieroglyphics)

Classical Antiquity (Greco-Roman World) (800 BC–AD 455)

- Main Type of Indoor Structure: Stone and marble buildings
- Greatest Fear: Finding out that the marauders, whom you heard are coming soon to your town, are *not at all* a cool jazz band

- Greatest Contribution to Indoorsmanship: Roman numerals (used today in most movie sequel graphics and at the end of the credits to denote the year in an expanded format no one can decipher… Thanks, Rome.)

Middle Ages (Medieval Times) (455–1500)

- Main Type of Indoor Structure: One-roomed peasant houses made of sticks, straw, and mud, which families often shared with their animals
- Greatest Fear: Finding out that ancient armor really isn't your strong suit
- Greatest Contribution to Indoorsmanship: The hermit lifestyle (developed and popularized by monks and scribes)

Renaissance/Age of Enlightenment (1453–1815)

- Main Type of Indoor Structure: Urban coffeehouses where fresh ideas were exchanged

- Greatest Fear: Falling asleep on a ship in the harbor while playing hide-and-seek and waking up to discover you are crossing the Atlantic

- Greatest Contribution to Indoorsmanship: Uh…coffee, of course

Industrial Revolution/Early Twentieth Century (1815–1945)

- Main Type of Indoor Structure: Small tenements in urban areas; small farmhouses in rural areas

- Greatest Fear: Walking through the city and suddenly being doused with the contents of a freshly filled chamber pot being tossed onto the streets

- Greatest Contribution to Indoorsmanship: Cars with windows that roll up and close off the outside world

Mid-Twentieth Century (1945–1975)

- Main Type of Indoor Structure: Row houses

- Greatest Fear: Communists (also not a cool jazz band)

- Greatest Contribution to Indoorsmanship: Televised sporting events

Late Twentieth Century (1975–1999)

- Main Type of Indoor Structure: Doublewides, apartments, and suburban houses

- Greatest Fear: Missing the newest prime-time network music video by Michael Jackson (featuring Eddie Murphy) because you had an Amway meeting

- Greatest Contribution to Indoorsmanship: The remote control

Early Twenty-First Century (2000–Present)

- Main Type of Indoor Structure: Apartments that cost as much as your grandmother's home, flipped houses, and mothers' basements everywhere

- Greatest Fear: The collapse of Amazon after a global Wi-Fi shortage destroys society as we know it…and not being able to post to Instagram about it

- Greatest Contribution to Indoorsmanship: Before Steve Jobs died, the iPhone; after Steve Jobs died, the 90-inch 4K Ultra HD Smart Television with voice command recognition (which costs as much as the smallest iPhone)

5. DEFINING THE ANTITHESIS— THE OUTDOORS

As with any discipline that has direct, oppositional challenges to one's desired mastery, it behooves a student to become familiar with the various elements of the adversarial position. The outdoors is most easily defined as "the area in the open air" or "those spaces outside of a shelter." In urban centers, many consider the outdoors to be simply the space between air-conditioned buildings.

Many cultural expressions and colloquialisms accompany the concept of the outdoors, usually ascribing to it attributes of greatness and beauty.

A. Common Expressions Casting the Outdoors in a Positive Light

1. The Great Outdoors
2. The Open Range
3. Fresh Air
4. The Wild Blue Yonder[2]

While there is most definitely a certain degree of wonder and beauty to the vast openness of the outdoors, many other aspects of the outdoors are less than

---

2. In this particular phrase, the adjective "wild," which generally denotes something uncouth or undesirable, instead invokes a sense of excitement and exhilaration.

desirable, if not downright dangerous. Such dangers have also elicited various labels for the outdoors that are often celebrated in today's culture for the sense of excitement and adventure they incite.

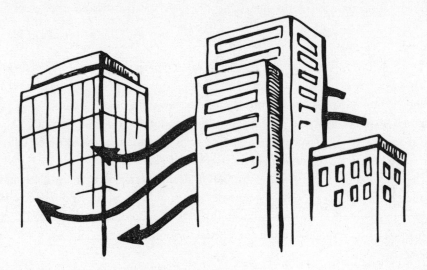

B. Common Expressions Casting the Outdoors in a Realistic Light

It should be noted that most people only admire the following seemingly adventurous aspects of the outdoors from the safe distance of their computer's screensaver, television screen, Instagram account, or couch.

The Wild Frontier

Unlike its grammatical cousin "The Wild Blue Yonder," this use of the term "wild" tends to create more of a warning or hesitation than the aforementioned idyllic invitation to dive headfirst, as it were, into the unknown treacheries of the outdoors.

No-Man's-Land

If a man were to jump out of an airplane with a parachute, should he ever intentionally attempt to land in an area so plainly and aptly dubbed? By virtue of its very name, no man should land in no-man's-land, man.

Wilderness

It is rare that someone intentionally travels into a true wilderness, except for the purpose of intentionally facing difficulty with the goal of allowing this difficulty to be a fulcrum upon which the viewpoint of one's perspective of life is tilted or altered.

Desert Island

Somehow this is a destination people often cite in their own "wildest dreams" scenarios, yet it is also the most common example of a place to be stranded for life with no hope for rescue. This should not be confused with a "dessert island," which would indeed fulfill the ultimate dream scenario for many people. This is but another of the unfortunate results of an ill-informed, undereducated culture that often interchanges the spelling of *desert* and *dessert*.

To that end, as our society continues to decline, one could say we are reaping our just "deserts" in terms of graduation rates and educational proficiency. But such tragic trends notwithstanding, a desert island is a direct example of the misconceptions swirling about the concepts of the outdoors and, conversely, Indoorsmanship itself.

Cape of Storms

In August 1486 the Portuguese explorer Bartolomeu Dias set sail from Lisbon with a fleet of two small vessels and a cargo ship. His goal was to sail round the southern tip of Africa to find a seaward trade route to India. But as he was on his voyage, a tremendous storm forced his ships off course, eventually forcing them to enter a bay known today as Mossel Bay in order to reach the safety of land. He named the cape around which he had navigated *Cabo Tormentoso* ("Cape of Storms").

Eventually, Dias reloaded his ship to continue the journey, and when he did, he made a remarkable discovery. The very storm that had almost destroyed his entire expedition had actually pushed him around the southern tip of Africa—which was his goal in the first place. He had succeeded in finding a water route to India; he just did not know it at first because he was blinded by the storms. Dias renamed the cape with a title more accurate to its final value to him: *Cabo da boa Esperanza* ("Cape of Good Hope").

Such a change in perception—from Cape of Storms to Cape of Good Hope— personifies our faulty modern viewpoint of the outdoors. We idealize the difficulty of the outdoors, even ascribing different, positive names to what has often caused only great distress.

Not to stoke the coals of conspiracy, but it is at least plausible that Dias changed the name of the Cape of Storms for the purpose of commercialization. That is, he knew then what any good marketing specialist knows today—intense difficulty is not an ideal salesman. Dias and the Portuguese crown had much to gain from other would-be explorers and traders following Dias's lead around this difficult cape for the purpose of establishing new commerce with the Far East.

Dubbing this great outdoor challenge the Cape of Good Hope ensured that many more opportunistic, economically minded explorers would be willing to brave the perilous elements for the "good hope" of great profit that beckoned from distant lands. One could suggest that it was such misrepresentations of the true nature of the outdoors (no pun intended) that fueled European exploration, settlement, and colonization of multiple areas around the globe, including the Americas.

It should also be noted that many terms from the natural outdoors have been absorbed into our popular lexicon for the explicit purpose of expressing the most difficult of circumstances. Such terms and phrases include but are not limited to the following examples.

C. Other Common Terms Expressing the Difficulty of the Outdoors

1. Dire straits
2. Missing the forest for the trees
3. Dead in the water
4. In hot water
5. The calm before the storm
6. Don't beat around the bush
7. It's a jungle out there
8. Fan the flames
9. Don't make waves
10. It's all up in the air
11. When it rains, it pours

EVALUATING YOUR LEVEL OF INDOORSMANSHIP

Man is not made for defeat [indoors].
ERNEST HEMINGWAY

A wise person once said, "The journey of a thousand miles begins with a single step." It is a beautiful sentiment, and while this person may have indeed been wise, the sage was obviously not an Indoorsman. Indoorsmen generally seek to minimize their steps and conserve their indoor energies for other endeavors, such as turning on the natural gas (or propane) fireplace or brainstorming newer and cleverer Wi-Fi passwords to amuse future houseguests when they request them.

Like so many areas of life and living, it behooves the Indoorsman to recapture—and if possible, redeem—many of the popular expressions of a world seemingly tilted toward the Outdoorsman's way of thinking. What we really need is a new lexicon wherein the ways of the Indoorsman are not dismissed but rather celebrated for the beauty they so effortlessly espouse. So, then, perhaps a better aphorism would read, "The journey of a thousand megabytes produces a gigabyte" or "The journey of a thousand dollars will buy you half a MacBook Pro."

1. BEGIN AT THE BEGINNING

The original expression notwithstanding, it suffices to say that anyone who wants to grow must begin somewhere—and it must be where they really are, not where they think they are, where they wish they were, or where they hope to some-day be. An honest evaluation is the starting point for any successful endeavor. If you want to lose weight, you must first be willing to step onto the scale. If you want to gain weight, you must first be willing to step on the accelerator and get to Chick-fil-A as quickly as possible.

Survival training is the best example of this principle. Many a would-be Avid Indoorsman has *set sail*—or more appropriately, has *sat still*—to think about their prospective metaphorical *sail-setting* toward the higher levels of Indoorsmanship mastery only to find themselves sorely disappointed, if not physically and psychologically injured. It is rarely the case that they lack willingness, enthusiasm, or even courage. It is generally more an issue of training. One cannot simply decide one day to master the indoors without being properly trained and equipped to do so.

So, then, how much of an Indoorsman are you at this moment? While the answer may be difficult to face (just like stepping on the scale), honesty is the first step to retraining your mind and growing in any respective field of study.

2. THE INDOOREAGRAM

Below is a test that will help you begin this journey to authentic Indoorsman-ship. You should take this test at the beginning of your training, but return to it periodically to monitor your progress, and, hopefully, your growth.

A. Twenty Key Questions to Determine Your Level of Indoorsmanship

1. If you were to encounter a bear, what would be your first inclination?

   A. Eat the bear alive

   B. Run as fast as you can

   C. Make yourself "bigger" to attempt to scare the bear away

D. Reach into your backpack and look for snacks to share with the bear, hoping to deter his anger and possibly win his affection

E. Reach for your iPhone to use your Scare Away Bears app

2. What is your personal definition of exercise?

A. Climbing the tree in the woods in whose branches you also live

B. Working out with weights, combined with intervals of cardio

C. Staying generally active by making better choices, such as taking the stairs at work or at school

D. Buying a treadmill and displaying it in your bonus room next to your old Thighmaster, Shake Weight, and Bodyblade

E. Spending two hours shopping on Amazon for a treadmill while contemplating the possibility of listing your old Shake Weight and Bodyblade on Let Go or Craigslist (obviously, you're keeping the Thighmaster)

3. What is the greater danger to the advancement of a healthy society?

A. People moving out of the woods and into houses

B. The threat of nuclear war with various unstable fascist or communist regimes in the Middle East and Asia

C. Terrorism (domestic and foreign)

D. The decline of Bitcoin, even if you've never actually purchased any Bitcoins…and even if you suspect that "Bitcoin" is not a real word

E. The threat of a multifaceted, long-term, widespread loss of Wi-Fi connectivity

4. If forced to pick one, which of the following combinations of items, services, or amenities would you most easily choose to live without for six weeks?

   A. Amazon one-day delivery, LTE service, central heat and air-conditioning

   B. Chinese takeout, hand sanitizer, your Keurig coffee maker

   C. Bathrooms, soap (liquid or bar), hand towels

   D. Car, boat, sidearm

   E. Food, water, shelter

5. Which of the following would most likely evoke a scream from you?

   A. A dance around the fire as you eat the wild badger you just killed with your bare hands

   B. An intruder in your home

   C. A fender bender

   D. A power outage

   E. A Netflix malfunction on the night of a season finale

6. Which is the better use of your money?

   A. Kindling

   B. Investing in a tax-free Roth IRA

   C. The equipment and installation of a security system

   D. Buying Powerball tickets

   E. Upgrading to the newest iPhone, even though iPhones tend to disappoint you more and more with each new model while also ironically increasing in price

7. If you had to pick one of the following people from history to send to prison, who would it be?

   A. The author of this book

   B. Genghis Khan

   C. Henry VIII

   D. Edward Snowden

   E. Whoever coined the abbreviation LOL

8. Which of the following is your idea of an ideal day?

   A. Not being eaten by a panther

   B. Dogsledding in the Arctic

   C. Hiking in the Rockies

   D. Charter fishing in the Pacific

   E. Channel surfing in the nude

9. If you could take only one item with you on an overnight trip, which of the following would you pick?

   A. Every night is an overnight trip

   B. Deodorant

   C. Extra underwear

   D. Book

   E. Smartphone (with charger)

10. Which do you instinctively consider to be the smarter fruit or berry?

 A. Bearberry (aka kinnikinnick)—which you eat off of the forest floor every morning

 B. Tangerine

 C. Apricot

 D. BlackBerry

 E. Apple

11. Which of the following is more dangerous?

 A. Trespassers approaching your campsite (i.e., your home)

 B. Joining the military

 C. MMA

 D. Skydiving

 E. Bidding online when the seller has a poor rating

12. What is your favorite bird sound?

 A. A click with which you communicate with your best friend, Clucky the black-capped chickadee

 B. A cuckoo

 C. A chirp

 D. A cock-a-doodle

 E. A tweet

13. What does it take for you to like something?

    A. There's no time for liking things; there's only time for preparing before the nor'easter hits your tree house

    B. High levels of quality

    C. High levels of helpfulness

    D. High levels of entertainment

    E. High levels of witty and well-conceived hashtags

14. What embarrasses you most about your childhood?

    A. Old pictures of you and Papa Bear, which is not a nickname for anyone

    B. Old pictures of you in the bathtub

    C. Preteen acne

    D. Prom date choice(s)

    E. Your MySpace profile

15. Which of the following infuriates you the most?

    A. The existence of civilization

    B. Unreasonable tax laws

    C. Slow drivers during rush-hour traffic

    D. Inaccurate weather reports

    E. Being locked out of the network because you attempted to log in one too many times simply because you couldn't remember if the password was all caps, started with a capital letter, or required a rarely used symbol (!, #, %, &, etc.) somewhere in the keychain sequence, even though such symbols remind you more of the way censored curse words are written

16. If for some reason you had to choose a body part that had to be colored, which of the following would be your most instinctive choice?

    A. Green thumb

    B. Black eye

    C. Black beard

    D. Yellow belly

    E. Blue tooth

17. Which of the following makes you more suspicious?

    A. Those beavers and their incessant chatter while building that infernal dam of theirs

    B. A knock at the door from a vacuum salesman

    C. A letter from Publishers Clearinghouse

    D. A voice-mail informing you that you qualify for lower rates on your student loans (even though you don't have a student loan)

    E. An email informing you that you're the heir to an African prince's fortune

18. If your friends come over to hang out, which of the following would you rather they bring?

    A. A box of ammo

    B. A bottle of wine

    C. A board game

    D. A scented candle

    E. A laptop power supply borrowed either recently or long ago

19. With which aphorism do you most closely identify?

    A. Answer the call of the wild

    B. Take the bull by the horns

    C. Choose the road less traveled

    D. The world is your oyster

    E. Sweet and sour chicken tastes great reheated

20. What footwear do you spend more time wearing?

    A. Hiking boots

    B. Steel-toed work boots

    C. Running shoes or sneakers

    D. House shoes (or slippers, depending on how secure you are with yourself)

    E. Multicolored toe-gloved socks with grippers on the soles

3. GRADING YOUR INDOOREAGRAM

1. Transcribe your answers to the list below.

2. Ascribe the following numerical value to your answers:

    A = 0 points, B = 2 points, C = 3 points, D = 4 points, E = 5 points

3. Find the sum of the numerical values to determine your Indooreagram score.

4. Descriptions of each level of Indoorsmanship are provided below.

    Question 1:   Answer Given _____ = Points Ascribed _____

    Question 2:   Answer Given _____ = Points Ascribed _____

    Question 3:   Answer Given _____ = Points Ascribed _____

    Question 4:   Answer Given _____ = Points Ascribed _____

    Question 5:   Answer Given _____ = Points Ascribed _____

    Question 6:   Answer Given _____ = Points Ascribed _____

    Question 7:   Answer Given _____ = Points Ascribed _____

    Question 8:   Answer Given _____ = Points Ascribed _____

    Question 9:   Answer Given _____ = Points Ascribed _____

    Question 10: Answer Given _____ = Points Ascribed _____

    Question 11: Answer Given _____ = Points Ascribed _____

    Question 12: Answer Given _____ = Points Ascribed _____

    Question 13: Answer Given _____ = Points Ascribed _____

    Question 14: Answer Given _____ = Points Ascribed _____

    Question 15: Answer Given _____ = Points Ascribed _____

    Question 16: Answer Given _____ = Points Ascribed _____

    Question 17: Answer Given _____ = Points Ascribed _____

    Question 18: Answer Given _____ = Points Ascribed _____

    Question 19: Answer Given _____ = Points Ascribed _____

    Question 20: Answer Given _____ = Points Ascribed _____

                                           TOTAL: _____

Final Indooreagram Score (total sum)

If you scored between **0 and 20**, you are an **Avid Outdoorsman**.

If you scored between **21 and 40**, you are a **Social Outdoorsman**.

If you scored between **41 and 60**, you are a **Casual Indoorsman**.

If you scored between **61 and 80**, you are a **Moderate Indoorsman**.

If you scored between **81 and 100**, you are an **Avid Indoorsman**.

4. UNDERSTANDING YOUR INDOOREAGRAM SCORE

Before delving into the specific descriptions of each level, it will be helpful to evaluate your desire and willingness to grow in these areas.

A. What If I Don't Want to Change? (A History Lesson)

This is a common question among those exploring the Indooreagram for the first time. In fact, the world is filled with people who have no interest in changing. For them—and perhaps for you—the status quo is more than just the only partially

Latin phrase you are comfortable using in regular conversation; it is also the general state in which you wish to live. The truth is, no one can make you change.

Or can they?

History is filled with people who didn't want to change, and yet they did so for the good of themselves, their families, and indeed society at large. Most people do not know that at the end of the American Civil War, Robert E. Lee was supposed to sign the documents that would finalize the surrender of the Confederacy in an open field. But a rainstorm arose, and the fledgling cease-fire, along with all hopes for peace, were almost lost for good.

Thankfully, a Union infantry corporal—an unnamed teenage hero whose story has seldom been told—humbly suggested to Ulysses S. Grant that they move the signing of the surrender documents to a home adjacent to the field in question. It was there, in the parlor of Wilmer McLean's home in the town of Appomattox Court House, that the documents were signed that halted the bloodiest conflict in American history, mercifully sending thousands of young soldiers home to their families and bringing a long-awaited peace to the nation.

Many find the process of baseless speculation to be foolish, but the Indoorsman embraces it as a valid method to search for the answers to various mysteries of history and culture—and with the advent of incredible indoor devices and technology, speculation is abundantly available at his or her fingertips. To that end, it is speculated that eyewitnesses to the surrender of the Confederacy attested that, after signing the documents, the war-weary and decorated General Lee stood up, put on his faded gray hat, adjusted his brass-laden officer's saber, and spent several minutes gazing at the walls and ceilings of the house. He then remarked, "I like it in here. Why have we been outdoors all these years?" Without another word, he left the house and never returned to war again.

Did he want to surrender? No. But was he glad he did? Probably not. Even so, should individuals today be forced to adapt to an Indoorsman mind-set? The historical evidence speaks for itself. Without the efforts of a young Indoorsman to influence a reluctant general, we might very well still be fighting the Civil War today.

B. What Does My Indooreagram Score Mean?

Again, most personality profiles circulating today among the fields of psychology and sociology, as well as social media, podcasts, and the popular culture at large, tend to focus on the discovery of one's most authentic self for the purpose of accepting this truest self. Yes, this is a bit overgeneralized in the sense that most of these also seek to help individuals find paths toward growth and avoid paths toward deterioration.

So as you read the following descriptions of the varying levels of Indoorsmanship reflected by your Indooreagram, realize that you are not learning about your truest self but rather just where you reside at this present moment. The goal is to see this version of yourself morph into another self, preferably one that is higher on the scale.

There is no need for shame during this process, even if you barely register on the scale in the first place. As we will continue to learn, many influential men and women throughout history found their way to lives of importance by becoming more adept at Indoorsmanship. Stick with it and be true to your future self.

Level 1: Avid Outdoorsman

As a general rule, stereotypes should be avoided, but when it comes to Outdoorsmen, they are fun and can save a lot of time. To that end, the Avid Outdoorsman often feels lost, mainly because he finds his way by watching the stars, listening to the ground, and using a compass to navigate. So his sense of feeling lost is understandable, mainly because he is.

General Description

Outdoorsmen live their lives seeking to connect with the outside world, which ironically disconnects them from the "world." It is this fundamental difference in the definition of the world that defines their inadequacies. The Avid Outdoorsman sees the world in a literal sense; that is, he sees the world as a planet and all the natural elements and inhabitants that populate it. While this definition certainly describes the world in a certain sense, it falls tragically short of the fuller paradigm of all that our world entails.

By solely focusing on that which is outdoors to the point that one reviles and ridicules the indoors, there is a separation from reality that grows with each passing experience. One begins to internalize—and indeed believe—that the outdoors is the purest expression of the world.

The greatest evidence of the self-deception expressed in an Outdoorsman's perspective is that, while he claims to love all things outdoors, he generally only seeks to experience a version of the outdoors that is isolated from people, such as a secluded hike in the Rockies or a weeklong bear hunt in Alaska. In each of these cases, the Outdoorsman's goals only work with small groups of people or in total isolation.

If the beauty of the outdoors is truly the pure motivation of the Outdoorsman, then walking through the crowded streets of Mexico City or Jakarta should be an Outdoorsman's dream, as there is an abundance of the outdoors present in such places. So, then, it is really not the outdoors that Avid Outdoorsmen are seeking but more so an isolation from people—and in some sad cases, their spouses and children. It is not a disdain of technology or the comfort of the indoors that truly motivates them, despite what their T-shirts and bumper stickers claim. It is a desire to be alone.

A desire to be alone is not at all a negative one. What Outdoorsmen really need is an education on the intricacies of the indoors that can offer them their most desired goal, but without the dangers of falling trees, poison ivy, and imminent attack by wild animals.

General Characteristics

- Prefers the outdoors to the indoors.
- Avoids coming in out of the rain (despite the famous expression and its implications in terms of one's common sense).
- Commonly inquires about hashtags, mainly wondering why everyone keeps using pound signs.

- Prone to bathe significantly less than the average human, but slightly more than the average animal.

- Is unaware that such things as fashion trends even exist.

- May pronounce Wi-Fi as "Wee-fee."

- Refuses to use a match to light a campfire, opting for more primitive methods, such as rubbing sticks together or using a flint and steel.

- Is prone to miss the forest for the trees by literally missing the forest (i.e., experiencing emotional detachment) when separated from the forest because he loves the trees so much.

- When he hears media warnings about protection from identity theft, he envisions someone breaking into his house, stealing his steel-toed boots and camo, masquerading around town in his truck, and wearing a fake beard, telling everyone, "Hey, I'm Eddie! Naw, I really are! Can I borrow 50 bucks?"

Pathway to Growth

The Avid Outdoorsman is not an animal even though he may smell like one. He is a member of humanity and should be respected as such. Ironically, his pathway to growth begins just as his path into the woods does: by finding the trailhead.

Below are five specifics of how he or she can begin the long journey to rehabilitation.

FIVE BABY STEPS FOR AVID
OUTDOORSMAN GROWTH

1. Make a vow, as difficult as it may be, to never again possess, for any amount of time, any vessel that contains urine of any kind, animal or your own.

2. Stop visualizing what every animal you see, including your family pets, might look like mounted on your wall.

3. Acknowledge that camouflage is not a primary color, nor should it be the main color in your wardrobe (also thus acknowledging that you actually have a wardrobe, whether you think so or not).

4. Stop using your Buck knife instead of dental floss, mainly because it's not working, but also because you are definitely filling your body with harmful bacteria.

5. Repurpose your fishing vest and its many pockets to act as a method for keeping up with all the remote controls in your living room that you keep losing because you can't figure out how to properly hook up or sync your devices to a universal remote.

Level 2: Social Outdoorsman

The term "Social Outdoorsman" is a bit of a misnomer because true Outdoorsmen generally strive to avoid those social connections that most members of society accept as commonplace, except perhaps those found in smaller groups on hunting trips, frog gigging expeditions, fishing tournaments, boat shows, impromptu meetings of strangers in the grass at interstate rest stops, and occasional taxidermy parties.

General Description

So the term "Social Outdoorsman" should not be taken literally but more so in the sense of someone who desires to project an image as an Avid Outdoorsman without the crippling social separation from society. The Social Outdoorsman enjoys the allure of the Outdoorsman's aura among the culture; that is, he wants to be considered rugged, self-reliant, knowledgeable of various survival skills, and generally in touch with the great outdoors. Indeed, he dabbles in each of these areas by taking a couple of hunting and/or fishing trips annually, although he is rarely successful on these outings.

You will find him in many pictures of groups of Outdoorsmen who are collectively displaying a large number of deceased waterfowl. In such instances, no one can ascertain who actually bagged how many, and that is just fine for the Social Outdoorsman. As long as he is a part of the tribe, his chief objective is being met.

General Characteristics

- Loves the idea of the outdoors more than the outdoors itself.
- Spends a lot of time and money at stores like Bass Pro, Camping World, and REI, but mainly purchases items as a collector rather than as an enthusiast.

- Feels no need to have a truck in order to be an Outdoorsman, despite the fact that his mentor, the Avid Outdoorsman, actually looks down on cars from his giant suspension-lifted diesel.

- May drive a hybrid, even a Toyota Prius.

- Decorates his automobile with the trappings of the outdoors so that everyone knows how Outdoorsman-like he is. These include decals with hikers and bumper stickers that make pithy jokes about hunting and fishing being more important than being at home, making a living, or caring for one's family.

- Is certainly aware that fashion trends exist—and thinks that camouflage puts him into an acceptable social class in terms of fashion (despite conventional wisdom).

- Is perfectly fine using matches, lighters, or even small blowtorches to light a campfire, desiring the benefits of the outdoors more than mastery of the primitive techniques required to survive therein.

- Instinctively jumps at the sight of insects, then looks around to make sure no one saw him before regaining his dignity.

Pathway to Growth

Like the Avid Outdoorsman, the Social Outdoorsman is not an animal, but he does run in herds. He sees the outdoors as beautiful and ideal, not necessarily as something to be conquered, but rather to be experienced and enjoyed with others. If the facade is removed (and if he acknowledges the existence of and agrees to engage in abstract thought), he will admit that the outdoors is really only the setting of his internal hero story, not the hero itself. While the Avid Outdoorsman seeks the wild adventure of the outdoors in the *outback*, the Social Outdoorsman seeks a more moderate experience of the outdoors as the *backdrop*.

FIVE BABY STEPS FOR SOCIAL OUTDOORSMAN GROWTH

1. Stop being jealous of the natural shine in the Avid Outdoorsman's beard—he doesn't want to offer you advice on what product he uses. He only cares about animal products.

2. Realize that playing hunting and fishing video games proves that your heart really desires the indoors more than the outdoors.

3. Wash the excessive mud from your Prius that you've left there to make people think you recently went mudding. You're not fooling anyone.

4. Rid yourself of shame in concentrated doses by talking openly about your hobbies other than outdoor hobbies. You like painting with watercolors. It's okay.

5. Stop flexing every time someone touches your arm.

Level 3: Casual Indoorsman

The Casual Indoorsman is the most common of all Indoorsman types. He lives a life unashamed of the indoors, but he also possesses a limited and reasonable interest in the outdoors as well.

General Description

The Casual Indoorsman has his or her feet planted in two worlds. He loves his couch but he is not opposed to taking a run or mowing the yard. He likes to travel, but still unapologetically prefers the comfort of his own bed. He may even enjoy the view of the open night sky through the retractable moon roof of his car.

He also has no fear of using the technological advances of modern society to adjust the temperature within his house, which is directly affected by the temperature just on the other side of his door, namely, the outdoors. This is significant because Outdoorsmen tend to display alarming levels of anxiety about—and even angry resistance toward—adjusting the thermostat in a home to make it tolerable for those who live therein. He will claim that he is saving money on the utility bills, and this, indeed, sounds like a reasonable explanation. However, his logic is easily debunked when one simply examines the amount of money he spends on Outdoorsman gear—hunting gear, fishing gear, hiking gear, climbing gear, scuba gear, etc.—at his favorite high-end outdoors-driven specialty retail establishment.

But an individual can be identified as at least having darkened the edges of a thin threshold into Indoorsmanship if he or she demonstrates a willingness to adjust their thermostat in order to utilize the modern technology now available to heat or cool their indoor spaces for survival and, dare it be suggested, even comfort.

General Characteristics

- Is difficult to identify as either an Outdoorsman or Indoorsman by his attire or paraphernalia. He may wear a North Face jacket, but it is doubtful he would ever climb any sort of face, regardless of its directional position, simply because his life situation would never present such an opportunity.

- May drive a car, truck, or SUV for practical reasons related to his actual daily life.

- Understands the basic principles of the technology of his indoor space, but he does not necessarily feel proficient in attempting any major troubleshooting or repairs.

- Prefers outdoor activities that are more related to sports or exercise than hunting, fishing, trapping, or survival.

- Attempts to contribute to conversations that involve either outdoors or indoors by listening to context clues, nodding his head, and occasionally offering an opinion.

- Owns a respectable number of electronic devices but limits his use of them as he feels that too much time spent not in the real world can damage him emotionally as well as socially.

Pathway to Growth

For the Casual Indoorsman there is a sense of balance in appreciating both the outdoors and the indoors, but there is no strong love for either. He is a chameleon, adjusting to whatever his living situation or social situation may require. From his perspective, technology enhances life, but it is not life itself. He is not a *creature of comfort*, but he does not mind having some *creature comforts* in his life, most of which are offered via the trappings of the indoors. He engages with the general population of social media conversation, but he tends to use social media more for its original created intention: to interact, catch up, and generally connect with people he already knows by looking at their photos, reading their thoughts, and liking their posts.

BABY STEPS FOR CASUAL INDOORSMAN GROWTH

1. Adjust your budget to allot more money for tech purchases.

2. Ignore the criticism of the Avid and Social Outdoorsmen who berate you for your willingness to adjust the thermostat to keep your indoors space inhabitable.

3. Read at least one new book on Indoorsmanship each year (or buy another copy of this book and read it again; old copies are not trustworthy and should be passed on to used bookstores).

4. Try to post at least one thought to social media every week that is original to you and not a retweet or a repost of someone else's thoughts.

5. Though you are a chameleon, try to avoid speaking authoritatively on matters in which your knowledge is not absolute. Just because you look like you know what you're talking about does not mean that you do. Humility is the trodden path of the wise.

Level 4: Moderate Indoorsman

The Moderate Indoorsman has not reached an elite level of Indoorsmanship, but his skill and knowledge should not be dismissed. Above all else, the most identifiable attribute of the Moderate Indoorsman is the desire to learn.

General Description

The Moderate Indoorsman understands and adheres to a principle of continuing education and practice, maintaining a healthy humility coupled with an insatiable hunger to add to his knowledge and experience. Such reasoning is similarly shared by the Social Outdoorsman, albeit on the opposite end of the philosophical spectrum. Perhaps that is why both levels are merely a single category away from their respective avid classifications. Just as the Social Outdoorsman is constantly asking questions of his avid mentors, the Moderate Indoorsman shares this consistent inquisitiveness with his socially awkward and misguided counterpart. As one of the prerequisites to growth is to become comfortable with the idea that you have a long way to go in achieving your goals, for the Moderate Indoorsman, this actually means becoming more comfortable with the idea of becoming more comfortable.

General Characteristics

- Spends a lot of time and money at stores such as the Apple Store, Best Buy, GameStop, IKEA, HomeGoods, and the like, but much like the Social Outdoorsman, his purchases seem to be more about being seen as an Indoorsman; that is, he is a collector as much as he is an enthusiast.

- Purchases an equal or lesser amount of his day-to-day items needed for survival or entertainment through online methods or via apps on his or her computer or smartphone.

- May drive any vehicle, including a truck or an SUV, but is as or more concerned with the indoor amenities than the functionality of the automobile itself. Such features include heated seats, Bluetooth capability, GPS guidance, satellite radio, etc.

- Directly relates the size of his high-definition television to his value as a person.

- Is skeptical about updates to his iPhone or Android device because he knows that all of his favorite apps may not yet be compatible with the latest operating system.

- Has nothing against the outdoors but doesn't even pretend to have any skill or ability in the same, to the point of going toe-to-toe in conversations with Outdoorsmen, pitting his Indoorsman knowledge against theirs.

- Exudes a slight sense of entitlement and immaturity over indoor amenities, often becoming frustrated when incredible advances in technology, such as ice dispensers, Wi-Fi routers, and automatic garage door openers—things at which most people throughout history would marvel—do not work exactly as they are designed.

Pathway to Growth

For the Moderate Indoorsman, the pathway to growth is simple, but that does not mean it is easy. His or her goal is to reach the next level of Indoorsmanship and become a master rather than an apprentice. This is less like earning a diploma and more like being promoted in the military. One may be technically qualified, but only when he or she begins to consistently stand out with traits that are obviously exceptional will the jump to the next level occur, even if he or she is not aware it has happened.

But in order for this growth to have the potential to occur, the Moderate Indoorsman must focus on facing the entitlement that produces various amounts of frustration in their indoor experiences. Contrary to popular belief, frustration is not the best pathway to positive change. Again, this level of Indoorsmanship is so far past novice perception and skill that one cannot simply *do* what they think should be done. They must also *think* differently. The road to mastering one's indoor *space* begins with mastering one's indoor *self*.[1]

FIVE BABY STEPS FOR MODERATE INDOORSMAN GROWTH

1. Restart your computer at least once a week. Whatever problem you're dealing with will probably be fixed through this technique.

2. Remember that staying indoors all the time and playing video games does not an Avid Indoorsman make. You may be a hoarder or just plain lazy.

3. For guys, mix up your wardrobe to include more colors than just dark black or light black (which is actually gray), especially if you ever want to marry a real girl someday.

4. When your voice-activated remote does not work, stop screaming at it as if changing your volume is directly related to your remote's ability to change the TV's volume. You're better than this.

5. Stop referring to yourself as a "hipster" on any of your social media profiles or posts. Real hipsters don't point it out as they are too busy drying out their fruit or making homemade wine in the basement.

---

1. Note to inner self: This is not an actual road.

Level 5: Avid Indoorsman

The Avid Indoorsman is a rare breed, and locating him out "in the mild" is something few people successfully accomplish. This is mainly because he keeps his doors locked, especially at night. But if one can ever gain access through this hinged gateway to the indoors (i.e., the door), behind it awaits a master of his domain whose life choices and life skills evoke deep insight and admiration.

General Description

The Avid Indoorsman makes the indoors; it does not make him. He lives and moves through life with quick-witted intentionality, using various aspects of the indoors as the backdrop for his creativity, efficiency, and pursuit of a sense of health in every aspect of his being, not just the physical. This holistic approach to life means he is not easily rattled when storms arise, mainly because he is safe and dry within his indoor domain. But also, in the metaphorical sense of storms, he is not easily rattled.

The Avid Indoorsman and the Avid Outdoorsman obviously live their lives at the opposite poles of their concept of the world. In the Outdoorsman's case, this pole is closer to the actual poles of the planet in that they are dangerous and largely uninhabitable. But, again, the Outdoorsman defines the world in terms of the physical attributes of the actual earth—that is his worldview.

The Avid Indoorsman, on the other hand, ironically internalizes a much larger viewpoint of the world, but he views it through a much smaller, more focused lens. Certainly, he does not deny the existence or value of the outdoors, but he sees himself as the next steward in line to advance the historical movement of humankind from the beginning of time, namely, in the great migration of life from the outdoors to the indoors.

If the Outdoorsman's motto is "The world is your oyster," the Indoorsman's might be "The world is your oyster cracker." While the oyster is considered a delicacy to many, it is also labor-intensive to retrieve, prepare, and (depending upon the particular preparation) consume. Also, you would never sprinkle oysters over a bowl of soup or open up a bag of oysters to snack on as you sit in bed and watch Netflix. Like the Outdoorsman's viewpoint of the world, it may not suit everyone's tastes—and smells.

But the oyster cracker is simple and inexpensive, yet so valuable in its own right. Much like the Avid Indoorsman's approach to life, the oyster cracker only enhances experiences; it never detracts from them. It can be successfully sprinkled across most anything. It is useful, accessible, and often overlooked in its simplistic brilliance.

General Characteristics

- Prefers a temperate climate and thus lives with a daily sense of gratitude for the modern marvels of HVAC systems and thermostats, by which he can actually dictate what the climate will be.

- Can effortlessly recite, in passing, ten significant differences between Uber and Lyft.

- Thrives on technology and is generally more adept at understanding it than the average person.

- Values privacy from the outside world by creating an inside world, wherein self, friends, and family can safely gather.

- Is often labeled an introvert, but this can be a misunderstood oversimplification reflective of his *habitat* more than his *habits*.

- Thinks frog gigging is merely an outdoor concert in the rain rather than what it actually is. Regardless, he would prefer to do neither.

- Contrary to popular belief, he is not afraid of roughing it and may even occasionally go camping with his family or friends, but as a master of Indoorsmanship, he will re-create many of the comforts and advantages of the indoors in whatever outdoor space he finds himself.

- Possesses an effortless, almost instinctive ability to seamlessly assimilate the latest app (and whatever service it provides) into his daily life, which means with a few clicks on his phone or even a few voice commands, he can order and have delivered to his doorstep anything he wants or needs in life, often having it arrive on the same day.

- Lives his life according to a moral compass, unlike his Outdoorsman counterpart, who is more likely to live his life following an actual compass.

- Technological devices and software seem to know and respect him in a way they don't interact with lesser Indoorsmen, resulting in an absence of errors, phone freezes, program crashes, and all the other general malfunctions of technology that tend to plague everyone else in society.

- Is an early adopter—if not a beta tester—for new devices and software, which includes an enthusiasm for the latest updates that cause problems for all other device owners and users. Because of this, the Avid Indoorsman is virtually immune to viruses and all other tech disasters.[2]

- Is the hub of knowledge for all his friends, family, and often even strangers for issues with their technology, which can cause him to sometimes feel overwhelmed and compel him to screen his phone calls.

- Sometimes experiences phantom phone vibrations even when he does not have his phone on him at all.

Pathway to Growth

When one has reached the level of Avid Indoorsman, the idea of personal growth may appear to be needless and foolish. But the Avid Indoorsman himself would disagree with such a conclusion. When one considers the nature of his avidness, the reasoning behind his need for growth becomes abundantly apparent. His mastery is of a fluid discipline, not a static one.

Indoorsmanship itself entails so many things that are constantly changing. Just in terms of technology alone, literally tens of thousands of updates happen every day. And consider one's most personal indoor space: the home, which may be

---

2. He, however, is not immune to real viruses of the medical variety.

stationary in terms of geographical location (except in the cases of RVs or mobile homes), but it is not static, because everything within it is in constant motion. From the internal workings of each appliance to the invisible network signals constantly balancing the entrances and exits of users, the indoors is in a constant state of movement and change.

Ergo, an Avid Indoorsman recognizes that a sense of humility coupled with a strong desire to learn and an unshakable work ethic are the keys to remaining a master of the indoors. Much like the apps on one's phone, which, when neglected to be updated, will eventually run slower, lock up, or stop working altogether, a true student of Indoorsmanship will always be searching for the latest update.

Furthermore, just like his phone or laptop, he will always be searching for the best network as well. From a human perspective, this means he will constantly be looking for and surrounding himself with like-minded Indoorsmen who will share their latest insights on technology, social media trends, general indoor philosophy, and the like. Unlike the Outdoorsman, who tends to shy away from human interaction, the Indoorsman welcomes it, although with very specific caveats related to his desire to best utilize his time and efforts in the presence of those who will challenge, sharpen, educate, and enrich his life as an Indoorsman.

FIVE BABY STEPS FOR
AVID INDOORSMAN GROWTH

1. Stay hungry. Continue to display humility and tenacity as you pursue a greater mastery of the indoors. Complacency leads to device malfunction, which is a law of the indoor universe. Also, stay hungry for food too.

2. Instead of screening your calls so much, sit down and have honest conversations with people, setting appropriate expectations regarding how much time you will be able to talk them through their technological issues and still maintain a healthy life.

3. Take vitamin D supplements (after consulting your physician first, of course), because your excessive time spent indoors is making your skin

look pale and pasty, which is why your mother keeps asking you if you are having regular bowel movements. Yes, the logical connection seems confusing, but in this case, vitamin D can indirectly cure at least the appearance of constipation.

4. Fight the urge to communicate solely via technology; that is, discipline yourself to meet others in person, look people in the eyes, and use your actual voice (this especially applies to your spouse).

5. Take time to remember things or figure out problems before you immediately reach for your phone to Google those issues. Your brain could benefit from having to add simple numbers, recall things you learned in history class, or figure out how to put together furniture without a YouTube video outlining each step.

THE INDOORSMAN VS. THE OUTDOORSMAN

If you talk to a [outdoors] man in a language he understands, that goes to his head. If you talk to him in his [indoor] language, that goes to his heart.

NELSON MANDELA

I t is advantageous to one's training to explore the seemingly adversarial relationship between the Indoorsman and the Outdoorsman. There is an assumption that one tribe is adamantly and diametrically opposed to the other, but such thinking is steeped more in hearsay and stereotypical rhetoric arising from cultural clichés than any solid, factual research.

1. DIVERSE PERSPECTIVES

The truth is that being an Avid Outdoorsman and being an Avid Indoorsman are not mutually exclusive paradigms of thought or living, although distinct differences can be observed between the two. Some view these two schools of thought as different ends of the same power button, each important to the functioning of society.

A great way to remember this integrative concept is the standard *I* and *O* buttons on certain devices, especially in Europe. Many Americans are confused by what these stand for, attempting to come up with various words beginning with *I* and *O* to determine which one means on and which one means off. Some think that *I* must mean "initiate," while *O* means "off."

But the truth is, these symbols are actually binary in nature, which means they are not letters but rather numbers. Thus, *I* is the number 1, which means something is turned on, while the *O* is the number 0, which means something is turned off.

In this vein, one can think of the *I* as the Indoorsman, or the philosophy that brings energy to one's way of living. Conversely, while there are times when one needs to turn something off, the *O* can represent the Outdoorsman, which refers to situations where there is actually no electricity and thus, in many ways, no hope.

2. THE DEFINING LIGHT OF LANGUAGE

One does not have to be a trained linguist or even speak more than one language to understand that words and phrases used in common dialects cannot always be directly translated. This is why, if you ever travel abroad, asking for something very simple in your native language can produce a seemingly complicated-sounding translation into the language of the region in which you are traveling.

Simply put, language generally does not translate word for word but rather thought for thought or idea to idea. For example, in English, one would say, "I am hungry." But in Spanish this same thought is expressed in a different order of thought and word. Instead of "I am hungry," the Spanish equivalent is "I have hunger": *Tengo hambre.*

In much the same way, a vast array of words and phrases in the English language have various and often diverse meanings when evaluated from opposing Indoorsman and Outdoorsman perspectives. Since Avid Indoorsmanship entails so much more than merely talking the talk, it is important that you know the deeper, often hidden meanings behind the words, phrases, and expressions you use. By developing a more complete and critical awareness of the Indoorsman's ever-developing dialect, you will grow in your comprehension as well as your ability to communicate these concepts to others who are seeking growth or mentorship in this field.

3. INDOORSMAN VS. OUTDOORSMAN INTERPRETATIONS OF COMMON EXPRESSIONS

Below are just a few common phrases whose meanings are completely different when filtered through either an Indoorsman or Outdoorsman perspective. Descriptions of these examples follow.

- Troubleshooting (vs. Trouble Shooting)
- Being Left to His Own Devices
- A Slippery Slope
- Outstanding in His Field (vs. Out Standing in His Field)
- Cliffhanger
- Breaching a Firewall (vs. Breaching a Fire Wall)
- Hacking
- Don't Poke the Bear
- Stable Employment

A. Troubleshooting (vs. Trouble Shooting)

Indoorsman Interpretation. Very few words or phrases so expressly reveal the philosophical chasm that exists between the Indoorsman's and Outdoorsman's way of life as the word *troubleshooting*. For the Indoorsman, this word means trying to ascertain the cause of a malfunction or problem, usually occurring with an appliance, device, or something else technological in its design, although certainly the word has been widened in the greater culture to include more abstract applications (i.e., troubleshooting problems in a relationship). From an Indoorsman's perspective, the purpose of troubleshooting is to discover a problem so it can be remedied or repaired.

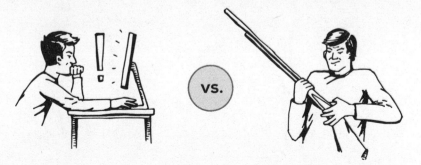

Outdoorsman Interpretation. The Outdoorsman interprets "trouble shooting" as something else altogether; that is, the act of having trouble while shooting. This means he is experiencing a malfunction with his firearm, crossbow, or compound bow, which can be caused by any number of variables. In the case of firearms, having trouble shooting has been experienced by Outdoorsmen going back multiple generations. In the early days of firearms, it could have been the result of damp gunpowder being placed into a musket, failure of a flint to spark when the trigger mechanism was engaged, or even the random explosion of the firing mechanism, causing damage to the firearm and also injury to the Outdoorsman using it.

B. Being Left to His Own Devices

Indoorsman Interpretation. For the Indoorsman, the interpretation of devices is completely different from that of the Outdoorsman, even though there is a similarity in outcome. In both cases, the person in question is left alone, but for the Indoorsman, there is no insinuation of scheming, ploys, or the like. It is much more literal, simply meaning that the Indoorsman values his or her time on a device such as a smartphone, tablet, or television. To leave him to his own devices simply means to respect his desire for a little solitude now and again to catch up on social media or simply to amuse himself with funny GIFs or YouTube videos.

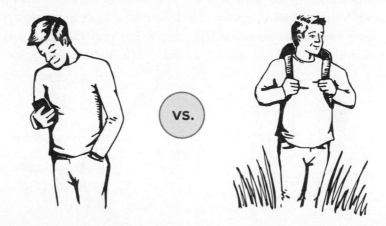

Outdoorsman Interpretation. This particular expression carries striking similarities in interpretation between the two perspectives in that in both cases it denotes a desire to be left alone in some capacity. The real difference is found in the meaning of the word *devices*.

For the Outdoorsman, the word *devices* in this expression carries with it something less akin to a literal interpretation and closer to an abstract viewpoint. It would be best defined as a ploy, a dramatic literary tool, or a scheme. So, then, the expression "leaving someone to his or her own devices" means "to let somebody do as he or she wishes" instead of giving the person direction or assistance.

C. A Slippery Slope

Indoorsman Interpretation. For the Indoorsman, this phrase is not literal but is obviously understood to be an idiom. This should be expected, as the Indoorsman tends to avoid situations in the outdoors where there would be anything slippery or sloped. To him, this phrase simply means that a decision, path, comment, or relationship may lead to difficulty in the future, as in the case of a metaphorical foot unexpectedly slipping on a metaphorical slope.

Outdoorsman Interpretation. For the Outdoorsman, slippery slopes are commonplace. The amount of time he spends outdoors leads him to traversing diverse terrains, including crossing rivers and streams and climbing and descending mountains. When he begins to walk or climb back down from an elevated position, especially depending upon the climate and recent weather patterns that may cause the terrain to be wet, muddy, or icy, it is common for the slope to become slippery, causing him to lose his footing and possibly fall to the bottom of the hill, mountain, or crevice being navigated.

D. Outstanding in His Field (vs. Out Standing in His Field)

Indoorsman Interpretation. Indoorsmen are often high achievers, studying hard in their respective fields and advancing to positions of leadership and prominence. As instinctive troubleshooters (see previous entry), they face difficulty and change with a remarkable sense of emotional elasticity and fortitude. They are undeterred (or are deterred to a much lesser degree, depending upon the avidness of their Indoorsmanship) by the onslaught of technological and communication issues that plague the world and the workplace to the extent that they are sought out as champions who can resolve whatever issues arise.

For these reasons, they are often recognized by their employers, managers, directors, and the like for their outstanding work performance. So to be "outstanding in one's field" means to excel in one's job or area of study, which means *field* is defined in the abstract sense as a subject, area, topic, discipline, theme, or domain.

VS.

Outdoorsman Interpretation. For the Outdoorsman, the phrase itself changes slightly as the interpretation moves to a more literal plane.[1] For him, he may also

---

1. This literal plane is, ironically enough, not a literal plane in the sense of aircraft but rather a more realized level of reality.

pursue the same level of excellence in his respective course of employment or study, and because of his predilection for the outdoors, this will often entail him actually being "out standing in his field."

Again, this is not meant to diminish in any way the intentions or efforts of the Outdoorsman, but his heart is more bent to the literal definition of a field as a meadow, pasture, grassland, ground, countryside, or lea. Such a field is a perfect place for tracking or hunting various animals, including certain fowl that can be rustled by a hunting dog while the Outdoorsman is out standing in the field, giving directions to his canine companion to retrieve the most recent prey.

E. Cliffhanger

Indoorsman Interpretation. Indoorsmen are students of culture and storytelling. With a propensity for being comfortable indoors and for using various forms of technology, the Indoorsman is no stranger to the finer points of the concept of narrative and all that it entails. In many ways, he is the counterpart to the ancient Greeks who analyzed the depths of setting, character development, exposition, climax, and resolve.

To that end, the Indoorsman can generally be successfully engaged regarding the ongoing story lines of the most popular television shows and movies being shown at present. Early twenty-first-century Indoorsmen are always up to speed on classic stories, including that of the both geographically and relationally confused characters of ABC's *Lost*. Many other shows could be referenced here, but suffice it to say that the Indoorsman knows them much better than the Outdoorsman. This attention to the detail of story continues with each passing year and with the advent of more and more stories—and the Indoorsman stands (or more likely sits) ready to discuss these with whoever approaches him in person or online.

So he knows that a cliffhanger is an emotional, often shocking, unresolved ending to an episode or season of a show or movie—one that requires resolution in the next episode or movie. This is one of the areas of life in which the Indoorsman can lose his cool due to the emotional anguish or excitement that can result from a cliffhanger, especially when a show is being watched from week to week as opposed to being binged via a streaming service.

Outdoorsman Interpretation. The Outdoorsman is also familiar with cliffhangers, but the stakes are much higher for him, sometimes including his very life itself. In the case of this particular interpretation, the definition of the word is explicitly stated within itself: actually hanging from a cliff.

Some extremely avid Outdoorsmen are known to climb steep rock faces and mountains without the safety of ropes or equipment. This is rare *and* dangerous. Most Outdoorsmen who attempt to do any sort of climbing do so in groups and use climbing equipment, such as harnesses, helmets, gloves, carabineers, and tightly wound rappelling ropes. In these cases, a cliffhanger can still cause great excitement, but more so for the purpose of entertainment rather than survival.

F. Breaching a Firewall (vs. Breaching a Fire Wall)

Indoorsman Interpretation. It is rare for anyone who is in charge (or even just simply working part time) in the fields of networking, IT, or web design *not* to be an Indoorsman, even if only as an amateur. Thus, the term "firewall" is very familiar and very important to these people, because they know it to be a critical, digital line of defense for their companies. Furthermore, they are often tasked with installing and monitoring these firewalls, which are features of a computer system or network designed to block unauthorized access while still permitting outward communication.

A breached firewall means that a nefarious online foe has found a way to break through whatever online security measures are in place for the purpose of stealing proprietary and/or personal information or possibly planting a destructive virus that can erase or corrupt all the information, records, and systems of an organization or its employees.

To the Avid Indoorsman, a breached firewall is a life-and-death situation, presenting a clear and present danger that must be faced with swift and definitive action in order to quell the malicious aggression of online enemies.

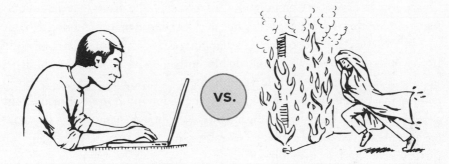

Outdoorsman Interpretation. The Outdoorsman is generally completely unfamiliar with the Indoorsman's concept of firewalls. In fact, most Outdoorsmen sleep soundly at night under the stars, never knowing that somewhere in a control room or a back corner office, a brave Indoorsman is actually saving the world by battling against the online attacks of enemy governmental regimes and the madmen who lead them with iron fists. The Outdoorsman's ignorance is no doubt bliss as he struggles to know how to plug in his computer, much less access the unseen digital wars that rage all around him.

For the Outdoorsman, though, there is significance to the idea of a "fire wall." For him, it means that a wall has caught fire inside whatever overnight lodge he is visiting or lean-to shelter he has constructed while hunting or camping. As many of these types of shelters do not have electricity, much less fire alarms, his awareness of the fire wall results from waking up to the smell of smoke and witnessing such a wall consumed in flames.

Much like the Indoorsman, a fire wall is a life-and-death situation to the Outdoorsman as well—perhaps even more so. In these situations, he will remember his training as a child regarding what to do during a fire. First, he will get low to avoid inhaling the smoke. Next, he will surround himself with a thick blanket (preferably a wet one, which is one of the only times the term "wet blanket" is used in a positive manner). In this case, the term "breaching the fire wall" means the Outdoorsman has no other choice but to run headlong into the flames so as to break through the burning wall and reach survival on the other side.

A couple of interesting observations can be made regarding the Indoorsman and Outdoorsman perspective on firewalls (or fire walls). The first is that the Indoorsman is attempting to repel a breach, while the Outdoorsman is attempting to create a breach. Second, the Indoorsman is attempting to better guard his indoor world from would-be intruders who would do him and others harm, while the Outdoorsman, as always, is attempting to leave the indoors as quickly as possible. It is also no surprise that breaching a fire wall only serves to reinforce the Outdoorsman's faulty assumptions about the danger of the indoors, even though, in most cases, fire walls are caused by a careless or foolish safety mishap on the part of the inhabitant—in this case, the Outdoorsman himself.

G. Hacking

Indoorsman Interpretation. Much like the breach of a firewall, the Indoorsman is no stranger to the hacker, which is a nickname for a person who uses computers to gain unauthorized access to private data. The hacker is the individual who is attempting to breach the firewall. Other nicknames for hackers include cybercriminals, pirates, computer criminals, keyloggers, keystroke loggers, hacktivists, and cyberpunks (the last being the Indoorsman's personal favorite nickname for these ne'er-do-wells).

The reality of the world of hacking for the Indoorsman is that he is going up against another qualified Indoorsman, just not of the avid persuasion but rather the evil persuasion. If the Indoorsman were a superhero, the hacker would be his archnemesis—his powerful, bizarro opposite and equal. The hacker must be taken seriously because the very survival and welfare of the indoors—and thus society itself—is at stake. This is why there are billion-dollar industries as well as dedicated government agencies staffed with professionally trained Avid Indoorsmen to vigilantly repulse all the advances of our cyberenemies.

So, to the Indoorsman, hacking is nothing to sneeze at.

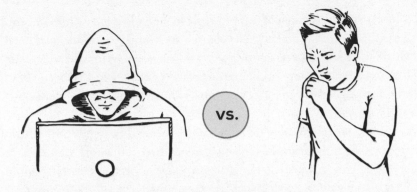

Outdoorsman Interpretation. For the Outdoorsman, however, hacking is absolutely something to sneeze at, literally. In his colder, bacteria-laden outside world, hacking has nothing to do with computers, cybersecurity, or the fate of the modern age. Rather, it has everything to do with the development of a nagging cough resulting from exposure to cold or wet weather, as well as from compromising one's immune system by extreme fatigue resulting from waking up to fish or hunt before sunrise for weeks, months, and even years on end. His persistent cough is often referred to as hacking or a hacking cough.

All this being said, the Outdoorsman's definition of a hacker is a far cry from the Indoorsman's definition. This is definitely one of those cases in which the two definitions should never be mixed, for obvious reasons.

H. Don't Poke the Bear

Indoorsman Interpretation. This lesser-known colloquialism is mainly used in the southeastern and midwestern United States, but it is still one with which Indoorsmen should fully familiarize themselves. It means that when something is seemingly going well, it should not be overengaged. By doing so, even if one's intentions are good, one can disrupt a delicate equilibrium that may never be recovered.

Other expressions that may be more familiar that express a similar imperative include "Don't upset the apple cart" and "Just leave well enough alone." The central message is, "When things are going well, it is wiser not to intrude into the situation with too much unnecessary change."

The most relevant example of this principle in the Indoorsman's life concerns the presence of children as well as adults who are not normally around children on a daily basis. Parents usually recognize the fragile balance of peace that sometimes randomly occurs when groups of children are playing together. It is a rare and beautiful thing, like a light snow in June or a double rainbow occurring simultaneously with a solar eclipse.

The point is, when children are at peace, they should be allowed to remain unfettered by outside interruptions and distractions. Even if there are a few screams here and there, Avid Indoorsmen know all is well as long as the screaming diminishes quickly and is not followed by children entering the adult space with tears or tattling.

Enter the well-meaning cousin, aunt, uncle, or grandparent. These kindhearted grown-ups can destroy the peace in a matter of seconds by entering the children's space, offering to help them find new games to play, inquiring if they are hungry or thirsty, or any other number of unnecessary engagements with the children. In this case, the children usually respond with crying, screaming, unreasonable requests, and a general sense of dramatic entitlement because their peace has been disrupted, thus reminding them to do the same for others.

Someone poked the bear.

Outdoorsman Interpretation. The Outdoorsman, on the other hand, interprets this expression very differently—and literally. Very few instances can be imagined in which one would be close enough to a bear to actually poke it with a stick or even a hand and, of course, even fewer logical instances for doing so.

Outdoorsmen take bears very seriously, which is why so many other expressions and references have arisen in their culture related to bears and bear behaviors. The protective nature of a female bear with her cubs causes Outdoorsmen to sometimes refer to any seemingly overprotective mother (even human) as acting like a mama bear. Other bear references include being as hungry as a bear, being smarter than the average bear, or giving someone a bear hug.

Outdoorsmen in the wild will often equip themselves to be ready to face any bears they may encounter. If they are hiking or camping in national parks or in other areas where bears are endangered or where firearms are prohibited, they will carry bear spray, a type of pepper spray or capsaicin that is used to deter aggressive bears in wilderness environments.

So, then, for the Outdoorsman, the idea of happening upon a bear and then deciding to poke it would be the most foolish action imaginable. Hunt it? Sure. Run from it? Perhaps. Poke it? Never. Though the paradigms and applications are different for the Indoorsman and the Outdoorsman, this particular expression actually carries similar meanings for both groups; that is, don't do anything unnecessarily stupid.

I. Stable Employment

Indoorsman Interpretation. This one hits close to home for the Indoorsman as he seeks to undo the gross stereotypes that plague his tribe. Many Indoorsmen, especially those of the millennial generation, feel unjustly characterized on social media and in the mainstream media as feeling entitled, unwilling to work at conventional jobs, and generally shiftless in their approach to employment, changing jobs over and over again when previous ones do not reach their unrealistic expectations.

But like most stereotypes, the ones levied against Indoorsmen are generally inaccurate. Indoorsmen are some of the most prolific and hardworking members of our society, especially considering that they often work to maintain the digital and technological infrastructures that keep that society intact and at peace.

So, for the Indoorsman, just because he may not be digging ditches, clearing forests, or pouring concrete does not mean he is not an indispensable member of the workforce. Stable employment, then, means a job—probably worked indoors—for which he is paid a fair wage and has the ability to move up the ladder (not to be confused with a job that actually entails climbing a ladder, which would probably not interest him). Rather, a job is considered stable if he can count on remaining employed for an extended period of time.

Outdoorsman Interpretation. For the Outdoorsman there is a similar interpretation of stable employment in the sense of a job that pays a solid wage with good benefits and longevity of opportunity. But there is also a chance that the Avid Outdoorsman would interpret this term as something else altogether.

It is entirely possible that stable employment could mean work done around farm animals, on a ranch, or, more specifically, in a barn. This is a stable job in the most literal sense of the word. And considering the disposition of the Outdoorsman, this kind of job could very well be exactly what he is looking for.

Such jobs include herding cattle, cleaning stables, training horses, or even working for a rodeo. Some may find it difficult to believe, but many Avid Outdoorsmen have found stable employment in the extremely volatile rodeo environment. It is a seemingly perfect combination of wild animals, outdoor recreation, danger, and living on the road, which satisfies at least part of the Outdoorsman's desire to live outdoors. In this particular case, the Outdoorsman can actually be applauded by fans and, in some cases, experience notoriety by being broadcast on various television rodeo shows both real and reality based.

While this may seem to be counterintuitive to the Outdoorsman's general aversion to extreme social interaction, there remains a sense of being a loner, especially if the Outdoorsman becomes a bull rider. All of the Outdoorsman ideals of ruggedness and fearlessness are sufficiently met in this lifestyle, or at least in this projected persona.

So while the Indoorsman seeks stable employment by working a long-term job from his computer or in an office area in which teams of people accomplish multiple tasks together, the Outdoorsman may seek stable employment by working as a farmhand, rancher, or even rodeo clown—also known as the roughneck clown, one of the unique versions of clowns that exists.[2]

In other words, even if an Outdoorsman is somehow forced to wear makeup, he is going to wear it as ruggedly as possible in order to satiate his inner desire to mirror the harsh outdoors as much as possible through his life—and even his appearance.

Of course, this would not be the first time Outdoorsmen have worn some sort of makeup, although they would never call it that, opting instead for the more resilient-sounding "face paint." Face painting has been a mainstay of Outdoorsmen for millennia, highlighting the rugged facial features of Native American warriors, Scotch-Irish warriors, Asian warriors, Australian aboriginal warriors, and the like. One need only remember the blue war paint that Mel Gibson (portraying William Wallace) splattered on his surprisingly clean-shaven-for-a-warlord's face in the movie *Braveheart* to recognize that, to the true Outdoorsman, there is a major difference between makeup and face paint.

To that end, unless one desires a slow and agonizing death at the tip of a bloody saber or the head of a huge mallet, it would probably behoove him never to approach a face-painted warrior—or even a clown, for that matter—before a battle or a rodeo to compliment his "makeup"—even if it does bring out his eyes.

Just leave it alone…that is, don't poke the bear because this is a slippery slope.

---

2. Check other reputable resources, Indoorsman or otherwise, to learn more about the many various types of clowns.

THE GREATEST DANGERS
OF THE GREAT INDOORS

Nothing in all the world is more dangerous than sincere
[indoor] ignorance and conscientious [indoor] stupidity.

MARTIN LUTHER KING JR.

The stereotypical Outdoorsman is portrayed as someone who is rugged, tenacious, and in possession of a personal proficiency for difficult, uncomfortable, and generally uninhabitable surroundings and situations. But like most stereotypes, what appears as easily observable data should not be carried out to foregone conclusions too prematurely. Each individual is unique and possesses varying degrees of outdoor and indoor mastery. And, yes, these masteries are possessed simultaneously.

1. DIFFERING PHILOSOPHIES
AND COMMON FEARS

Many sociological theories postulate that stereotypical Outdoorsmen—those who spend all their spare time sleeping under the stars, hunting in the wild, or sailing the open seas—are actually running, even if only subconsciously, from an inner fear of the indoors. These theories suggest the masculinization of the Outdoorsman veneer to be merely a facade veiling something else altogether, something deeply embedded in the Outdoorsman's deeply wounded soul.

What do Outdoorsmen have to be so trepidatious about? The obvious incredulous tone of the question reveals, at least in part, errors in perception between the two tribes. The assumptions that accompany Outdoorsmanship are tethered to a presumed sense of complete self-sufficiency and contentment, almost as if those who can conquer the wild frontier must also be in control of all the other important aspects of life.

If these particular assumptions carry with them a sense of pride, then their converse—the assumptions about Indoorsmen—carry the opposite: shame. Surely this should not be so, mainly because the pride and self-reliance of Outdoorsmen do not diminish the fear and shame they still feel when facing the elements of the indoors. Ironically, many common fears are commonly reported among the Outdoorsman and Indoorsman communities respectively, as addressed in detail below.

2. FOMA (FEAR OF MISCELLANEOUS ASSEMBLY)

Sometimes the anxiety associated with this category is referred to as FOMA (fear of miscellaneous assembly).

A. Kitchen Appliances

Though little assembly is usually required for ovens, stoves, microwaves, or refrigerators, these appliances are bulky, heavy, and often involve gas lines and electrical wiring, which can contribute to the Outdoorsman's anxiety.

B. Bathroom Fixtures

Faucets require a minimal amount of assembly, but the directions must be followed to a T if one is to avoid the emotional devastation that accompanies the discovery that the hot and cold handles were assembled either incorrectly or on the wrong sides.

Toilet assembly provides its own unique level of stress due to the delicate nature of the purpose of the apparatus itself. Even if a toilet is new and has never been used, there is something unnatural about touching various parts of it, especially the outer rim. Even Avid Outdoorsmen find toilet assembly to be a less-than-desirable task.

C. Indoor Furniture

Furniture assembly presents a uniquely infuriating level of challenge to the Outdoorsman and the amateur Indoorsman as well. When applicable, the size of the box in which furniture arrives is proportionate to the level of Indoorsmanship required to conquer the task of assembly with minimal profanity and/or fits of rage. In general, if a small box arrives for a large piece of furniture, then the energy and time required to successfully assemble said piece will be much greater.

D. Miscellaneous Deck and Pool Paraphernalia

This is a unique category because, to the person who is not an indoor enthusiast, the area of the deck and pool would at first glance appear to obviously belong to the outdoors category. This is why more education is needed. A more accurate view is that anything physically connected to the home or situated for recreational purposes within 20 to 30 paces of the home should be considered as a part of the collective indoors of the property in question.

DOES IT HAVE A
PRIMARY INDOOR USE

A good rule of thumb is that an item outside the house should still be considered an indoor accoutrement if and only if it serves an indoor purpose, namely, something that not only *can* be done indoors but also generally *is* done indoors. A swimming pool is a great example of an indoor accoutrement because its main function—some form of bathing, albeit hopefully recreational in this case—is predominantly performed indoors in a bathtub. Indoor pools also reinforce the logic of this classification as well. Another example is a grill (gas or charcoal), because its primary function is to cook food, which in the modern age is predominately done indoors.

An example of an item that may be positioned within the allotted distance from the home yet should not be considered an indoor accoutrement is a trampoline. The telltale test for any item such as this is the simple question: Does this item have a primary indoor use? In the case of trampolines, it is obvious that they do not. Only in isolated instances, such as circus tents, acrobatic theaters, or recreational businesses that specialize in padded spaces for children, whereby excessive jumping is monitored for safety, would there be any need for an indoor trampoline.

Their categorization and respective usage notwithstanding, the assembly of deck furniture or pool accompaniments should not to be taken lightly, even if the objects in question are actually light in terms of weight.

E. Children's Toys Assembled on Christmas Eve

This particular FOMA is felt even by the most avid Indoorsmen, so it should be no surprise that Outdoorsmen often reel from it as well. None can deny that there is a unique and debilitating pressure that accompanies the process of assembling children's toys the night before Christmas.

Sleep deprivation is the most common detriment to successful toy assembly as well as the most acute cause of stress. In general, the Christmas Eve assembly process does not begin until the children have been tucked into bed. Of course, because it is Christmas Eve, children must often be revisited multiple times before sleep overtakes them, due to their excessive excitement over the pending yuletide celebrations as well as their listening for actual hoof and bell sounds on their roofs.

Another challenge for the assembler is the struggle to maintain a healthy mental focus. Besides sleep deprivation, this struggle often arises due to personal and familial stresses caused by the visitations of so many family members in a short amount of time. These holiday gatherings often rekindle seemingly forgotten yet still presently awkward conversations and stir up difficult memories in the process.

But the physical and mental challenges of the night notwithstanding, the most difficult ordeals related to Christmas Eve toy assembly are the toys themselves.

Much like furniture assembly, there is an important rule to consider in such situations: The age of the child is directly disproportionate to the number of pieces in the toy's packaging. This rule really only applies to toddlers and older kids, not to newborns, whose toys are really just for the amusement of the parents. But once a child reaches the toddler age, this rule can be and should be applied. What this means is that a one-year-old's toy will require a much higher degree of assembly than a ten-year-old's toy. While this seems counterintuitive, it is true.

A great example is a plastic toy kitchen for a two- or three-year-old girl. While one would assume that such an assembly process would be simple, nothing could be further from the truth. Opening the seemingly nonformidable box, a vast array of plastic pieces pour out onto the floor. Most of the pieces are still connected to a plastic mold and must be worked out until they break free.

At this point, anxiety levels begin to rise as the unassuming assembler comes to the dark realization that the directions contain inadequate and often inaccurate drawings obviously meant to confuse and disorient adults, which only adds to the timed pressure of meeting the Christmas morning deadline. Some choose, albeit unwisely, to proceed without using the directions at all. Such a desire is understandable, because the creators of the directions have obviously intended either spiteful jesting or downright harm to the reader. Even so, the directions are the only source of hope for successful assembly, even if they only provide isolated shreds of information that must be pieced together, translated, or decoded into a somewhat discernible vernacular.

Remember that as children grow older, the number of pieces in the assembly process of their toys declines. As young boys and girls begin receiving dartboards or Nerf guns instead of unassembled motorized Power Wheels (which come as a pile of plastic pieces, unchargeable batteries, and endless sticker pages) or unassembled art easels (also known as a box of wood scraps), the necessary assembly is minimal.

Thus, at this stage of toydom, the real challenge shifts from assembly to the process of unboxing the toys in question. To this day, scientists are uncertain how various toys, such as action figures or Barbie dolls, are so overly, even impossibly secured into their plastic or cardboard packaging. In some cases, it has been reported that there have been as many as two to three thousand plastic or rubber-banded connections per square inch of certain toys, each requiring separate, meticulous cutting before the toy can be successfully detached intact from its commercial entombment.

Various conspiracy theories about this issue are gaining credibility among many sections of the Indoorsman community. Some claim these impossibly thorough packaging processes are, in actuality, clandestine attempts by the Chinese government (possibly aided by several black ops agencies of the Russian Federation) to thwart American growth and development by contributing to the decline in the mental health of its citizens. In other words, these packages are like Trojan toy horses designed to unseat the emotional confidence—and also the sociological fortitude of the family unit itself—among the unsuspecting victims who are tasked each holiday season with removing these toys from their cardboard confinement.

A recent study revealed that removing action figures from their packaging is considered to be only slightly more difficult than writing a bestselling novel and slightly less difficult than passing the bar exam in the state of Mississippi. So, while assembly is lessened, an untrained attempt at unboxing can actually require an even greater amount of time and, subsequently, frustration.

This is one area where Outdoorsmen find a successful cross-training of their skills in terms of Indoorsmanship. This is mainly because they are usually familiar with the use of knives. This comes into play because the best course of action in removing a toy from its packaging is to address the package with a dual approach of knives and scissors. A classic blunder is to attempt to use these tools to remove the toy from the front (toy facing up). Such an approach causes both frustration and likely damage to the toy itself, especially when the doll or action figure has excessive hair, which can be easily cut by mistake when attempting to reach the plastic or rubber connections holding the toy captive.

The best approach is to turn the box over (toy facing down). From this angle, you must resist the temptation to give up after seeing the unnecessarily cruel and excessive amount of tape covering the ends of the plastic and rubber connectors. This tape need not be removed, only slit in places with the knife so as to release the pressure of the packaging. After some strategic cutting has exposed the connectors, you may use the scissors to easily snip them. This approach keeps your respective blades from damaging the toy, and it also reveals the location of the connectors without the distraction of the toy's accessories, which often obstruct one's view when the toy is facing up.

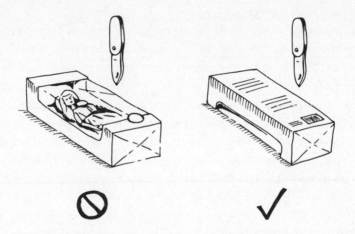

The only other challenge here is when there are twist ties. Do *not* attempt to cut these; they have a metal strip at their center. The only course of action is to cut away the tape and then manually untwist the ties until they release. Safety and sanity must be your highest priorities.

F. Children's Toys Assembled on Christmas Day

This act of Indoorsmanship is very similar to the previous section, thus all the previous directives should be applied here as well. The main difference is that assembly on Christmas Day must be done in the presence of those who have received the gift as well those who are waiting to play with the gift. One should not underestimate the amount of emotional pressure the assembler may feel under the watchful eyes of so many parties.

Take extra precautions when dealing with aunts or uncles who desire to appear cool in the eyes of your children. There are many reports of these adults intentionally purchasing presents for their nieces and nephews that require an extremely difficult and lengthy assembly process, as well as higher levels of noise. They seem to find a special enjoyment in watching a struggling parent attempt to unpack and assemble a highly complicated toy as previously described, all the while being pressured by onlooking children who have no sense of patience—and perhaps also only a modicum of basic humanity.

Some psychologists refer to this phenomenon as "Holiday Hypnosis"—a state of mind in which excessive receiving of gifts combined with high levels of sugar-laden foods and the complete suspension of any regularity in routine and schedule produce an alarming alternate state of mind, which is characterized by extremely high levels of entitlement, which is manifested in unreasonable demands for more gifts and unpredictable emotional outbursts, often reaching tantrum levels.

It is no wonder that even the most prepared Outdoorsman can become agitated, irritable, and perhaps nauseous when facing the Christmas Day assembly process. The best course of action, besides following the above instructions for the removal and assembly processes, is listed below.

Four Keys to Successful Christmas Day Toy Assembly

1. *Remain calm.* Breathing deeply will help, but be careful not to appear to sigh in frustration, as such actions can offend onlooking family members, including your spouse, grandparents (especially if they purchased the toy in question), and, in extreme cases, the child for whom you are assembling the toy in the first place—even though they are seemingly dazed and confused in a state of holiday hypnosis.

2. *Utilize the directions, even though they appear to be (and actually are) worthless.* Yes, as you've already learned, the directions will no doubt be filled with flaws and pitfalls, but never forget they are a treasure map, not a road map. In other words,

you will have to piece together various clues by using deductive reasoning and dumb luck in order to solve the mystery in enough time to keep holiday hypnosis from souring the children and adults around you.

3. *Be mindful of sharp objects.* Many amateur Indoorsmen fail to realize the level of chaos a Christmas Day present-opening moment can produce. Of course, you will no doubt need to use the aforementioned knife and scissors, but always remember that small children will be darting in and out of your periphery with little or no concern for their own safety or even conscious awareness of which planet they are living on.

4. *Avoid eye contact with onlookers until the toy is fully assembled.* Although there will be those who think they are helping you with the assembly process, their suggestions and insights can prove to be distracting and perhaps even detrimental to the assembly process itself. On many occasions, such advice has led an assembler to snap, cut, or adjust a toy in such a way that permanently damages it, which can also lead to permanent damage in the family relationship "for whom the toy tolls," so to speak. Stay on task and avoid adding too many cooks to the toy kitchen.

Assembly can be a challenging area of Indoorsmanship worthy of increased study and intentional practice. One suggestion is to create an assembly range (not to be confused with assembly *of* a range) in your home and practice putting together various items as a timed exercise. If you really want to grow in your craft, special order unassembled items from China or—for more advanced Indoorsmen—buy some furniture from IKEA.

The important thing is to remain an eager student of assembly and never assume you are a master with nothing more to glean. Such arrogance is the beginning of your downfall. Yes, confidence is a key to successful Indoorsmanship, but great Indoorsmen maintain a healthy respect of the indoors, constantly reminding themselves that, at any moment, things can change (especially if the indoors in question is an RV or a mobile home).

3. THE INDOOR FEAR OF REPAIR

A movement is afoot in our society to subcontract all indoor repairs out to trained or qualified professionals. This shift is yet more evidence in the decline of healthy Indoorsmanship among the nuclear family unit. Historically, repairmen were only summoned to face extremely specialized and difficult situations, such as replacing a roof or installing a gas line.

If there is one area where Outdoorsmen and Indoorsmen alike tend to cringe with anxiousness, it is the area of repair. But this need not be the case. All that most indoors enthusiasts need in order to gain competence for repairs around the house is a little training in two specific areas that tend to challenge even the most advanced Indoorsman. Yes, there are many other areas of repair besides these two, but research shows that most of these areas can be addressed with the confidence to try—as well as access to the internet, where simple Google searches can be performed.

A. Repair Problem 1: Plumbing

There may be no other greater challenge to the mental acuity of the Indoorsman than an unanticipated plumbing emergency. And the truth is, even the smallest of plumbing projects can feel like an emergency. At the root of the issue is the presence of liquid and its insistence on remaining undammed by whatever man-made system is attempting to contain or channel it.

Indoor plumbing itself is an unbelievable testament to the advancement of the Indoorsman's mission across the various eras of history. Obviously, running water and indoor sanitation systems are considered modern advancements, but this is simply not the case. In terms of human action producing access to water, ancient wells believed to have been dug around 6500 BC have been discovered in the Jezreel Valley, a large fertile plain and inland basin south of the Lower Galilee regions of Israel.

But how long ago did early Indoorsmen design their homes with access to water and sanitation? The answer may surprise even the staunchest Indoorsman skeptics. Skara Brae was a Neolithic village in Scotland near Orkney in which archaeologists have uncovered indoor plumbing, including water-flushing toilets. This plumbing apparatus was a crude two-channel stone system lined with tree bark and designed to channel fresh and wastewater in and out of the houses, respectively.

Asian societies, such as the Indus Valley civilization, also learned the art of indoor plumbing as early as 2350 BC. In the Indus city of Lothal, all houses featured private indoor toilets. These wastewater systems were connected to a covered brick sewer system, which had been installed using a gypsum-based mortar. These sewer lines led out of the city and into the surrounding bodies of water, or in some cases into cesspits dug for such purposes.

What is the significance of all this? Such knowledge assures us that ancient Indoorsman were taking on plumbing repairs somewhere between 3180 BC and 2500 BC. Therefore, modern Indoorsman can be encouraged to confidently paddle through the troubled waters that plumbing repairs may release upon them.

That said, all plumbing repairs are not equal in their challenge or skill level. Let's address a few of the most common areas of greatest frustration.

Toilet Repairs

In the previous chapter, in the section on assembly, the hesitation of the assembler was addressed regarding toilets because of the less-than-desirable business that occurs in (and sometimes upon) them. The only saving grace for the Indoorsman during assembly is that the toilet is new and thusly unsoiled, unless something very strange and unorthodox has previously occurred at the hardware store or the supplier from which the toilet was purchased. Even so, this grace is completely neutralized when it comes to the area of repair because, if a toilet needs repair, then it has no doubt been used—and possibly abused—often.

Toilet Clogging

Toilet clogging should not be confused with *artistic clogging*, which is an expressive style of American dance with origins in the folk dances of the British Isles, Africa, and pre-Columbian America. On the contrary, toilet clogging is much less entertaining and generally involves a more pungent odor, depending upon the

severity of the toilet clog or the quantity and personal hygiene of the dancing cloggers.

Regardless, toilet clogging is the most common repair most Indoorsmen will face, and it is not for the faint of heart or the squeamish of stomach. You will first notice that a toilet is truly clogged when, after multiple flushes, the toilet bowl (complete with all its recently deposited contents) continues to fill with more and more water, showing no signs that any of the contents are being released into the sewer or septic line at the base of the toilet.

Some Indoorsmen will struggle to determine that a toilet has truly been clogged until the situation has escalated into a full-on crisis, which can include flooding of the contents onto the bathroom floor, allowing sewage to settle into any carpeted areas and also seep beneath doors and into the surrounding hallways and rooms. In most cases, such a crisis could have been avoided if excessive flushing had not occurred, but the perpetrator of the clog often slips into an alternate, panicked state of consciousness known as clognitive dissonance.

Clognitive dissonance (CD) is characterized by extreme anxiety, nervous-based perspiration, wild fanning of arms and hands in the air (trying to dissipate the foul stench), a loud and obviously forced cough (meant to cloak the embarrassing sounds of excessive flushing), and a profound sense of shame. Those suffering from clognitive dissonance are difficult to observe in their inflamed condition, as their identity often remains unknown. Those who create toilet clogs often try to escape detection by quietly slipping out of the bathroom and into the general population of the indoor space.

In extreme cases, the person who discovers the clog is usually blamed for the clog, even if such blame is never explicitly levied against them by the other occupants of the greater indoor space. But the emphatic insistence by the person who discovered the clog that he or she is *not* the one who caused it, coupled with the fact that the actual perpetrator never speaks up, tends to raise suspicions to the point that everyone lets the blame fall, by default, upon the discoverer rather than the real perpetrator. The situation can quickly devolve into a classic case of protesting too much, or as it is often stated in a less-refined cultural colloquialism, "Whoever smelt it, dealt it." The sad truth is that discoverers are merely victims of their own need to use the bathroom, the clognitive dissonance of the previous occupant, and bad timing.

CD is a dangerous condition, as too much flailing of the limbs can produce muscle pains, cramping, or, in rare cases, the dislocation of one's shoulder. There is also an external danger of fire due to the fact that toilet cloggers are also known to strike matches in the enclosed space of the bathroom for the purpose of diminishing the smell.

The Avid Indoorsman knows the best path for the prevention or resolution of toilet clogs begins with complete honesty. If you have guests in your home, inform them all before they enter the bathroom that if they experience what they think is a toilet clog, they should simply find you so you can address the problem while calling as little attention as possible to the perpetrator. Honesty and openness can help everyone avoid an indoor crisis and prevent innocent bystanders from experiencing the ravishing effects of clognitive dissonance and the shame associated with it.

In terms of the actual repair, a simple plunger will generally do the trick.

Kitchen Plumbing Repairs

Not all indoor crises affect the whole population of the respective indoor space the way a toilet clogging incident will. In most cases, a plumbing repair entails the solitary efforts of one responsible Indoorsman, which means he or she is usually on their own to handle the crisis and return the indoors to the desired state of tranquility that all indoor occupants desire.

This is most true when it comes to plumbing repairs in the kitchen, namely, a leak under the sink. At first glance, a simple water leak seems like a minor incident, but research shows that more catastrophic fits of rage resulting in injuries or the intervention of law enforcement have been the result of simple water leaks than any other indoor repair.

The primary cause of this seemingly uncontrollable frustration stems from the act of unwisely believing the mirage that the leak in question is a minor problem. Such arrogance is yet another example of not adequately respecting the indoors. As you train to *master* the art of Indoorsmanship, if you do not properly respect the indoors, the indoors will become your *master*.

There is, in fact, no such thing as a minor leak. While small leaks may inflict less damage upon the surrounding cabinetry or flooring than large leaks, they can actually be more difficult to resolve. The reason is the minute nature of the problem itself; that is, a single drop of water repeatedly seeping, albeit tortuously slow, out of a seemingly sealed pipe fitting.

The common sequence begins with a household member discovering that the leak exists. This usually occurs when they reach under the sink to retrieve dishwasher detergent, a garbage bag, or a sponge. To their dismay, they discover the cardboard box that holds the dishwasher detergent pellets or the sponges is damp and disintegrating. Upon further investigation, more water is discovered, as most of the other items under the sink are saturated.

Some might say this discovery creates a "sinking" feeling.

If the Indoorsman is not the one who discovers the leak, he or she will be quickly called upon to intervene. All the wet items must be removed, many of which will need to be discarded due to the amount of water damage. The Indoorsman will be wise not to let the frustration over the financial cost of these wasted items set him or her on a downward emotional trajectory, especially at such an early point in the repair process. Yes, you may have experienced loss, but compounding it with the loss of your confidence or perspective will only cause the problem to worsen and fester faster.

If there is ever a time not to let the indoors win, if only for the moment, it is now.

After you have removed the debris and dried the leaked water, the next step is searching for the source of the leak. In many cases, the leak will be coming from one of the water supply lines, and most likely at the area of the fitting itself. Prepare yourself for a shocking surprise when you see such a small amount of water dripping at a tortoise's pace—you will be tempted to waste your time marveling at the level of destruction such a small drip has produced. But as you now know and don't have to waste time pondering, there is no such thing as a "small" leak.

This point in the process is where many amateur Indoorsmen make the deadliest mistake. It is so tempting to tighten the fitting to the point that the simple leak will simply stop leaking. Such an outcome is an illusion, if not a delusion. Obviously, you must turn off the water to the lines by turning the shut-off knobs at the base of the cabinet. But after this, *do not*—and let the point be repeated—*do not* attempt to repair the leak by simply tightening the fitting with a wrench. The temptation is understandable, because such action can be taken quickly, perpetuating the fantasy that the problem can be easily resolved.

But this will not solve the problem, no matter what your eyes tell you. In this case, you must walk by faith and not by sight and discount the notion that tightening the fitting will fix the leak.

Many wannabe Indoorsmen have attempted just such simple fixes. At first glance, it seems to work, stopping the microscopic leak and filling the heart of the repairer with a cruel sense of false hope. Part of the problem with such action is the nature of this particular repair endeavor itself. You will be lying on your back, with half of your body looking up into the darkness of the sink's nether regions, with your legs protruding across the kitchen floor. At first this position is sustainable, but the sharp corner of the cabinet below your back, acting like a sort of pain hinge, will quickly cause your discomfort to grow—and everyone knows that an uncomfortable Indoorsman is a sloppy Indoorsman.

A headlamp is the preferable light source in these situations, because holding a flashlight or a cell-phone light in one hand while trying to turn the fitting with the other is impractical and inefficient. But even if the space is well lighted, tightening the fitting is a dangerous game of cat and mouse. As you lie there with the

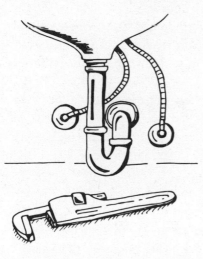

corner of the cabinet digging into your back, your mind will begin to play tricks on you and try to convince you that you are not seeing any more water dripping from the area of the leakage.

Yes, seeing water should be a simple act that any competent human or animal can successfully accomplish, but in the compromised state of the plumbing repair mind-set, you are no common human, or even animal, for that matter. The main confusion arises from the inability to discern if the water you are seeing is new or old; that is, whether it is freshly dripped or residual from the previous drippage. Again, time is of the essence because of the back pain that is increasing with each passing second.

Furthermore, when the Indoorsman is working alone on the repair project, he or she has to come out from beneath the sink to turn on the water above in order test the alleged repair. This up-and-down, back-and-forth movement will test the very fortitude of even the most experienced Indoorsman. At the end of the day, detecting the leak will be nigh impossible to do after simply tightening the fitting.

Some repairers attempt to use white plumbing tape on the threads of the fitting to seal off the invisible area where the leakage is occurring. This tape is certainly a valid tool for plumbing installation projects, but it should be used sparingly for plumbing repairs. By the time one has tightened the fitting, climbed up top, turned on the water, climbed back under, looked for the small leak, turned off the water supply, tightened the fitting some more, turned the water back on, climbed back up top, turned on the water, and so forth and so on for an hour, the mental and digital (literally, using your fingers) dexterity required to successfully use the plumbing tape will have substantially diminished.

Unlike most tapes, plumbing tape has no adhesive on either side. Its main use is to wrap the threads, thus creating a seal when the nut is tightened around them, compacting the tape into the tiny grooves of the fitting. This could work if one is able to unroll the correct amount of tape to wrap once or twice around the threads, without the tape folding in on itself. But in a compromised state of emotional and physical exhaustion, do not count on this tape to do its job. One can waste so many minutes—if not hours—wrapping, rewrapping, and unwrapping these threads after each unsuccessful leakage test.

Take note that this hypothetical leak repair saga can also occur outside of the kitchen. The most common equivalent is a leak in the water supply line to the toilet, which generally comes out of the wall just below and behind the tank. Every scenario listed above in the repair of a sink leak can also be expected in this case, notwithstanding the below-the-sink items that have been ruined by the previous leak. After all, most people do not store items beneath their toilets, except in rare and rather exceptional, if not disturbing, cases.

This exhaustive description of what can go wrong in this particular field of plumbing repair is only offered as a cautionary tale to help you avoid the madness that can ensue in such instances. The encouraging Indoorsman wisdom that can lead would-be repair persons away from such anguish is that when a supply line leaks, simply go to your nearest hardware store and purchase a replacement supply line for less than ten dollars. Yes, driving to the store will require time and effort, but in the long run (and even the long drive, as it were), it is well worth the trouble.

Replacement is the only logical, even merciful pathway to repair such leaks. Pride leads us to believe that we can see and fix the minor problem, but the truth is that the actual cause of the leak is probably microscopic in nature, measured in unseeable nanometers of space that have developed on the threads of the fitting in a place invisible to the naked eye, thus causing an indiscernible leak to occur.

Resist the urge to disregard this wisdom, because not doing so can cost you arguments with your spouse and family, hours of lost time, and in somewhat far-fetched yet quite possible scenarios, your very life.

B. Repair Problem 2: Doors

The importance of keeping doors in good repair should not be quickly or easily dismissed as they are, quite literally, the gateways between the indoors and the outdoors. The metaphors could pile aplenty, but time is of the essence. It suffices to simply point out a few grand moments in life and history when doors defined the magnitude of whatever event was occurring.

A Brief History of Doors and Their Importance

When young love blossoms, morphing to a lifelong commitment "until death do us part," countless traditions don the day with wonder and awe. The bride and groom often choose not to see each other until the moment when she emerges at the back of the venue in all her beauty—after all, that is why the phrase "a bride on her wedding day" is a thing.

Something old. Something new. Something borrowed. Something blue. The tearful speech by the maid of honor. The classic roasting of the groom by the best man. The hideous dresses picked by the bride for her bridesmaids—dresses that ensure she alone will be the sole focal point of the day. Flowers. Candles. Music. The bride being walked down the aisle by her father. The decoration of the car in which the happy couple departs the reception, which they climb into right after they are lovingly pelted in the face with rice and/or birdseed.

These customs and more are each worthy of the highest regard, but another tradition signifies more than just the ceremonial niceties. It is only after the groom picks up his bride and carries her across the threshold—literally through the door— of their new house that said house becomes a real home. It would behoove all brides and grooms to adhere to a few words of wisdom during this tradition if, that is, they want it to be memorable for the right reasons and not for the subsequent trip to the emergency room that can ensue.

First of all, the bride should wear clothes made of a fabric that doesn't easily slide. Otherwise, she may slip right through the groom's grip and onto the hard floor below. Second, the groom must remember to treat this lift with the same guidelines as any other (though he should refrain from stating anything of the sort out loud); that is, keep your back straight, lift with your legs, and in some rare cases, enlist the help of a friend. Of course, he should avoid any grimacing or expression of pain or anxiety before, during, or after the carrying of the bride across the threshold. If he does not understand this basic tip on his own already, it is questionable whether he should have pursued said nuptials in the first place.

But lest we forget, without the door, there would be no functional threshold— and quite possibly no marriages.

Another key thought about the critical importance of doors to life and society is their use throughout history. One doesn't have to be religious to recognize the name of Martin Luther. His efforts to courageously address the various abuses of the late medieval Catholic Church and restore an understanding of real faith to the common people in their own language were the very foundations of the Reformation. Historically, these events cannot be overstated in their influence upon the advent of the Enlightenment as well as the Industrial Revolution and modern society as we know it.

How did all this begin? Did Luther write down his ideas and post them on the largest tree in the nearest forest? Did he stand in the square and simply shout the truth to all who passed by? Did he make paper airplanes out of his theological viewpoints, letting the wind carry them where it would?

Of course not. He nailed his Ninety-Five Theses to a *door*. Only then were these positions recognized for the incredible insights they espoused.

So, then, when repairing a door, the Indoorsman must never underestimate the importance of the job at hand, even though it can be tedious and discouraging at times for myriad reasons, not the least being the weight of the door itself, which can make the repair process especially challenging. Perhaps this weight is merely a metaphorical reflection of the weight of importance that doors inherently bear.[1]

Indoor plumbing issues are only slightly more challenging than the repair of various issues related to either interior or exterior doors, but the Indoorsman should not underestimate the task. To be quite honest, most people walk right past doors or, more accurately, right through them with little or no thought about what is required to keep them safe and functional. It mustn't be so for the Indoorsman.

Unlike a water leak, a door problem usually takes much longer to be noticed because it slowly reveals itself over time. The most common problem that occurs with doors is uneven hanging.

---

1. Perhaps not.

Uneven Hanging of Doors

When a door is first installed, it is no doubt evenly hung within a leveled door-frame. But just because it is hung appropriately does not mean it will remain so for months and years to come.

Most people become aware of a door evenness issue when they can't get a door to stay shut, notice that the door is sticking, or can't get the dead bolt to lock properly. This problem is generally caused by one of three problems: 1) the normal settling of a house over time, 2) the problematic settling of a house due to structural issues in the foundation caused by water damage or faulty construction techniques, or 3) a drastic change in climate or weather conditions. On this last point, do not be surprised if there are seasons of the year when your doors hang unevenly and others when they do not. This is yet another occurrence that reminds us to develop and maintain a healthy respect for the indoors and all the mysterious phenomena that accompany it.

There are many ways to address an unevenly hanging door, but the best suggestions are to begin by making sure you have eaten a hearty meal, are fully rested, and have removed all small children from the house who may be too impressionable to witness the hurling of random projectiles or sudden outbursts of explicit profanity.

Once these precautions have been taken, address the door head-on and attempt to visualize the offset nature of its crookedness. If you look around the edge of the door, is the space equidistant on all sides, or are there greater gaps in some places? This process of checking the gap is crucial, as evidenced by its use in ancient societies to philosophize the meaning of life, the function of the soul, and the meanderings of the heart. Some call it gap theory. (Please note that the door gap theory is unrelated to the religious Gap Theory. Applying religious Gap Theory to an unevenly hanging door will not accomplish the Indoorsman's desired goal—though many have tried.)

Next, open the door. You will see the hinges, each containing three to five wood screws. If the door is leaning to the bottom left when it is closed, take a drill with an appropriate bit or an appropriate screwdriver and tighten the wood screws in the top hinge. This will hopefully cause the door to rise to the right and correct the problem of unevenness. Use similar techniques of tightening and loosening with each of the hinges, depending on the nature of the door's unevenness.

If this does not correct the problem, you might insert a small, thin piece of wood (known as a shim) behind one of the hinges in order to allow more room for the door to be square in its space again. This shim should not be confused with a shiv, which is a slang term for a makeshift knife or blade crafted out of everyday prison supplies (although working with a shim can make you want to stab somebody).

At any rate, using a shim will require removing the door from its hinges as well as whichever hinge you want to place the shim behind. After the shim is placed behind the hinge, you will need to insert the screws back through their holes and through the shim.

To remove a door from its hinges, take a small screwdriver or punch, along with a hammer, and tap upward on the smooth door bolts to gently drive them up and out of the hinges. Be careful, because this bolt and the hinge are often covered in

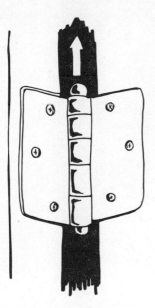

grease, which can stain and quite possibly ruin your clothing. (If at first you can't get the bolts to move, try having someone else lift up on the door a bit to relieve the downward pressure.)

Many an Indoorsman has experienced great frustration at this point because, in most cases, the door will come right off its hinges with no problems. But there are times when the laws of physics seem to unhinge themselves from reality easier than the door you are attempting to unhinge from the frame. Stay calm. Chew some gum to help relieve the pressure in your ears that has set in due to your increased blood pressure. Play some jazz music (either via an instrument, if you are capable, or simply through your sound system). Take a walk. Stay hydrated. Pet your dog. Light a candle.

Again, taking a door off its hinges should be a simple task, but at times it is not. That is why psychologists have developed the term "being unhinged" for the emotional state that can overtake the unassuming Indoorsman who is working on a door that refuses to come off its hinges. One way or another, something is going to come unhinged. Your goal is not to be it.

If you find yourself in this state or feel you are approaching it, it is best to *take* a psychological break rather than *experience* a psychological break. You must remain in control and be proactive if you wish to avoid waking up in a fetal position or worse. In fact, in the rare case that you do muster the courage to insert a shim, psychiatry consultation coupons are now available for free at most hardware stores. They are usually attached to the packaging of the door shims.

THE GREATEST DANGERS OF THE OUTDOORS

If people think nature is their friend,
then they sure don't need an enemy.
KURT VONNEGUT

Most people are more familiar with the dangers of the outdoors than the indoors. Even so, there is a benefit to at least acknowledging some of these dangers if for no other reason than to add credence to the reasoning behind the Indoorsman's superior alternative methodologies for daily living.

1. GENERAL CREEPING AND CRAWLING THINGS

As has been pointed out already, the outdoors is home for insects, snakes, and other undesirable creatures that strike fear in the hearts of children around the world. A true Avid Indoorsman does not avoid the outdoors out of fear of these things, but neither does he pursue the outdoors to intentionally face them. There are certain Indoorsmen who spend their time studying these outdoor creatures, but they often do so in an indoor (laboratory) environment.

A. Snakes

When it comes to snakes, most Indoorsmen possess a natural, instinctive sense of enmity toward these scaly belly crawlers. When encountered in the wild, some Outdoorsmen may intentionally get close enough to a snake to determine its species and thus also determine the level of danger it poses to everyone present. Often they say, "It's okay, everyone! It's just a garter snake!"

The Avid Indoorsman, on the other hand, does not trust the skills of the Outdoorsmen to quickly and, what's more important, *accurately* identify the type of snake that has been encountered. After all, the differences in appearance between one species of snake and the next can be minimal, and yet the differences in its ability to attack and kill its prey (including human prey) with a lightning-fast puncture from its fangs and the forced injection of its deadly venom could not be more *striking* (pun actually intended this time).

At any rate, wrongly identifying a snake is a game the Indoorsman would rather not play. And, yes, a game is an appropriate metaphor for this kind of experience, because there are children's rhymes about distinguishing one of the world's most venomous predators (the coral snake) from its harmless yet almost identical cousin (the king snake). The rhyme goes like this:

> *Red touch black, safe for Jack.*
> *Red touch yellow, kills a fellow.*

This rhyme teaches children that the coral snake will have bands of red touching smaller bands of yellow rather than black. But let's be honest. Many children are still learning their colors. Should we, as a society, be composing nursery rhymes about such things? And who would want to name their baby Jack after hearing such a nightmarish work of poetic cruelty?

At any rate, when it comes to snakes, the Indoorsman sees no color except red. That is, he very well may flee at the first sight of a snake in the wild because he is unlikely to trust appearances and has internalized the assumption that there really isn't time to stay and figure out if a snake is venomous or harmless. Or he may instinctively reach for the nearest sharp object with a handle and attack the snake with a wild fury that can be quite disturbing to witness.

In ancient Indoorsman lore, there is also a rhyme for what to do if you encounter a snake in the wild. The translation into English is rudimentary, but the general idea is as follows:

> *Eyes see snake, run and get a rake.*
> *Red, green, or black, whack, whack, whack!*

2. ALL CREATURES BIGFOOT AND SMALL...AND BIGGER

Beyond the realm of insects and snakes, dangers rise from the general animal population as well. Any of the regular programs on the Discovery Channel or Animal Planet can educate viewers to the dangers of the animal kingdom, so there is little need to do so here. Suffice it to say there are hazardous scenarios related to animals out in the wild.

For the purposes of the present study of Indoorsmanship, let's focus on two creatures that exclusively inhabit the outside world and are, for all intents and purposes, fully representative of that world itself.

A. Bigfoot

The creature known in North America as Bigfoot (and its counterparts and cousins) goes by other names around the world: Sasquatch, Skunk Ape, Yeren, Yowie, Mande Barung, Orang Pendek, Yeti, Barmanou, and Abominable Snowman.

Though many consider Bigfoot to be a mythical creature contrived in the paranoid or delusional minds of conspiracy-minded people, many individuals in the world—and especially in the Pacific Northwest—claim to have seen such a creature. Alleged witnesses have described it as a large, hairy, muscular, bipedal, apelike animal. It is rumored to be very tall, ranging between six and nine feet in height. It is also supposedly covered in black, dark brown, or dark reddish hair.

Is Bigfoot a legitimate outdoor danger? There's no way to really know—but yes. There is, however, a surefire way to avoid such a ferociously terrifying beast: Become an Indoorsman. Other than the 1987 family comedy *Harry and the Hendersons*, which starred John Lithgow, there is no record of a Sasquatch-type animal ever attempting to venture over a threshold and into an indoor space.

And yet even in this fictional tale of an unlikely friendship between the two species, Harry did not intentionally decide to enter the Hendersons' dwelling but rather was brought there after being struck by their station wagon, presumed to be dead, and then tied to the roof of the vehicle for transportation back to the suburbs. It's a tale as old as time. So, then, even in the movies the indoors is an unlikely place to encounter a Bigfoot unless you plan on rendering it unconscious with your car and transporting it there yourself.

B. Loch Ness Monster

The creature known as the Loch Ness Monster (or Nessie) is believed to be an aquatic animal of unknown age and origin that reportedly lives in Loch Ness in the Scottish Highlands. "Loch" is the Irish, Scottish Gaelic, and Scots word for lake. It can refer to a sea inlet, firth, fjord, estuary, strait, or bay.

This particular creature, as it has been described by those who claim to have seen it, is very large with a long neck and one or more humps on its back. These humps can be seen protruding from the water, much like the dorsal fin of a shark. The legend of the Loch Ness Monster grew to worldwide acclaim somewhere around 1933, when a photograph showing the silhouette of the creature was circulated in the Western media and subsequently appeared in a variety of books, periodicals, and newspapers.

Most of the scientific community, however, considers the existence of this particular being to be nothing more than folklore and completely lacking any biological proof. They relegate the purported sightings as the misidentification of other objects in the water due to poor visibility, subconscious self-deceptive imagination, or elaborate hoaxes conjured for the purposes of fame, money, and notoriety.

The Indoorsman's perspective regarding the Loch Ness Monster can easily be deduced by extrapolating the critter's last name: Monster. There are very few times in life when a monster is considered a good thing or something to be desired. In fact, the only instances that come to mind have to do—as they did in the case of

Bigfoot—with fictionalized works of cultural artistry in the realm of media. Such examples include animated movies like *Monsters, Inc.* and its sequel. But even in this case, one must recognize that besides the desire to make a profit from the production and propagation of such films in the marketplace, these movies were created to counteract the commonly shared fear of monsters in our society, especially among children.

So, then, if one only examines the cultural responses to the possible existence of monsters such as Nessie, it is easy to conclude that the real and rational opposite of the characters created in such movies are the most accurate representations of their real-world counterparts. In other words, if film producers try to reverse the common assumption about monsters by making them friendly, sympathetic, and relatable, then the common assumption itself is actually closer to the truth, namely, that real monsters, like the Loch Ness Monster, are unfriendly, devious, and desirous of the ruin of humanity. This logical sequence proves beyond a doubt the true nature of Nessie, no matter how many harmless nicknames it attempts to adopt for itself.

Because the Indoorsman shares a love for such logic, he would never see a need to come near such imminent danger. And, once again, this danger is completely neutralized, even more so than Bigfoot, by simply remaining indoors. Even if a dam were to break, causing a loch to flood a nearby town—and even if during this deluge, Nessie were to swim into a human dwelling—very few houses would be big enough to contain her.

Thus, it is not a far-fetched conclusion that individuals who own large houses or estates—and particularly those of ancient Gaelic descent who still possess medieval castles that have been passed down through generations—are in significantly greater danger of the Loch Ness Monster actually attacking them inside their homes.

If you fit this description, it may be tempting to live in a state of anxiety or fear of such an occurrence. But there probably isn't anything you can do to avoid it, except perhaps run for political office and make sure that your local lochs have modern locks and dams that are regularly inspected by engineers and receiving the appropriate scheduled repairs and maintenance. Besides this, the best course of action to survive a Loch Ness Monster attack in your home is to continue training yourself to reach new levels of Indoorsmanship mastery so that when the moment arises, you will react to it from a place of finely tuned instinct rather than high-pitched panic.

3. DIRT

It may seem a curious thing to list dirt as an outdoor danger, but Indoorsmanship thrives on a healthy curiosity—not the kind that killed the cat but rather the kind that helped the stray cat find a home indoors.[1]

Dirt is the most basic and primal reflection of the earth itself, even doubling as an interchangeable term as evidenced by English phrases like "turning over earth," which refers to digging or plowing the dirt.

So, then, dirt is literally the earth, and the earth unfettered by human progress is almost exclusively an outdoor thing. The only exceptions are the random shelters that naturally appear under the dense canopy of jungles or caves and caverns snaking their way beneath and through mountain ranges. Other than these isolated examples, most of the earth—including the dirt that covers it—is exclusively outdoors.

Dirt is literally the flooring of the outdoors. To walk or hike in the wild and find anything other than dirt underfoot (except perhaps rock, water, sand, or ice) is unheard of. It is an earthen reality as accepted as the earth itself is—the purest reflection of the planet's raw and rugged state.

---

1. Cats are not the pet of choice for the Avid Indoorsman. See chapter 8.

This is why Indoorsmen throughout history have resisted dirt with such vehement passion. To most people groups, dirt represents the separation of the outdoors from one's indoor space. In other words, it is where one flooring ends and the other begins—and to get dirt on your floor reveals that the outdoors is intruding into the indoors, removing the sense of safety and security one feels indoors.

Consider the fact that even when dirt is not technically involved, we still refer to something as "dirty." We define the opposite of clean by the basest substance the outdoors has to offer. The surface of a man-made piece of furniture or even an electronic device can be smudged or perhaps possess a tiny layer of dust, and someone will say, "Clean that now! It is so dirty!" The same can be said of children who haven't bathed in several days. It is unlikely (though not impossible) that they are actually ever completely covered in dirt, but even so, we will tell them how extremely dirty they are.

Is dirt a dangerous thing? Yes, it is, if only in the sense that dirt within an indoor space blurs the revered separation the space has from the outdoor space just across the threshold. Yes, only a few inches actually separate the outdoors from the indoors, but one cannot overstate the emotional miles spanned in those few inches. Crossing successfully into the indoors is like instantly teleporting to another realm wherein weary life travelers can find respite from the harsh world outside.

Dirt is dangerous because it threatens the integrity of this realm. The seriousness of this possible breach is easily seen by observing an Indoorsman who describes himself or herself as a "neat freak" or "clean freak." When said person finally collapses onto a couch or into bed after a long workday, their seemingly blissful state of rest can quickly be upended by the cursory discovery of something in the room or house that is dirty.

This person will instantly spring to his or her feet and let out a sigh of frustration and perhaps a few angry words in the direction of the person he or she believed was going to clean all dirt from the indoor space. Arguments often ensue. Feelings are hurt. Peace is lost. And in many cases, profanity is used—which is why curse words are sometimes referred to as "dirty words."

So, then, the delicate equilibrium of the family unit itself can easily be upset by the mere presence of dirt. It may not be a snake or Bigfoot, but dirt is a perilous deterrent to a peaceful indoor existence. Almost every culture recognizes this truth. Ironically, even cultures with dirt floors seem to have an aversion to dirt. In these cultures, men and women are often seen sweeping dirt more than cultures where indoor flooring is not made of dirt.

At first glance, sweeping dirt across a dirt floor seems to be counterintuitive, but nothing could be further from the truth. The reality is that most people groups instinctively possess a common aversion to dirt, especially in their indoor spaces. Thus, even people with dirt floors still sweep their floors, not so much to remove the dirt, but to more tightly pack the lower levels of dirt beneath the dirt. Over time, this dirt hardens and becomes a more solid surface. The result is a hard floor made of dirt that no longer possesses the physical properties of dirt, so much so that dirt can actually be swept off the surface of the dirt floor.[2]

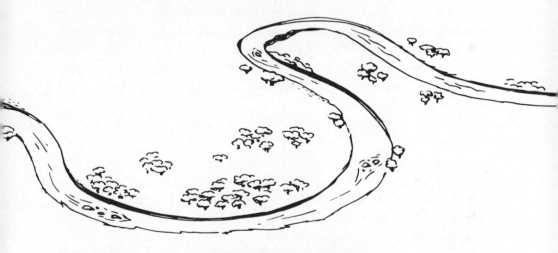

4. WATER DANGERS

As one of the most essential compounds to the human experience, water makes up almost three-fourths of the surface of the earth and two-thirds of the human body. Even so, for the novice interested in exploring danger, water sources are not the place to get one's feet wet, so to speak. It is nothing to be trifled with, as demonstrated by the following dangers.

---

2. Dirt dirt dirt…just seemed like a great chance to say dirt a few more times.

A. Rivers

The history of all human settlement follows the winding turns of rivers. The earliest known civilizations arose near an area that is known as the Fertile Crescent in the Middle East (not to be confused with the Fertile Croissant, a French country restaurant that specializes in breakfast and brunch dishes). The Fertile Crescent was situated between two life-giving rivers: the Tigris and the Euphrates.

The geography of rivers predicts the geography of settlements and cities because rivers provide fresh water for drinking, a food source in the fish they contain, more food sources in the animals and birds that also seek these fish, and a constantly moving force that keeps the waste moving away from the living spaces. Besides this, rivers provide a way to transport much-needed supplies for survival and for building.

The Indoorsman has a special respect for rivers because he sees their invaluable role in helping people create more indoor spaces through the process of settlement and community building. While there are dangers (such as drowning and flooding), the Indoorsman's philosophy is that rivers are the most helpful type of water source by which to situate one's indoor space or a congregation of multiple indoor spaces (i.e., a community or city).

B. Oceans

An ocean produces a different level of danger for the Indoorsman. While oceans provide an abundance of wildlife for food, salt water is useless for drinking. Furthermore, the possibility of hurricanes and typhoons threaten the structural integrity of indoor spaces, not to mention the supply of electricity—and, by default, Wi-Fi connectivity. Plus, there is a danger of pirates.

Indoorsmen often vacation near oceans, but only because the space they occupy is usually rented, which means that even if there is a major flood or wind damage to the indoor space, the Indoorsman himself will not be emotionally fraught with the weight of the incident nor liable for the repairs thereof. This gives him peace of mind as he—and many other vacationing Indoorsmen—inhabit the indoor spaces that dot the shoreline of many seaside communities.

5. UNPREDICTABLE WEATHER

Perhaps there is no more imminent danger produced by the outdoors than weather. Indeed, at the very heart of the drive of the human race to constantly move indoors and to make indoor spaces roomier, more comfortable, more efficient, and more capable of sustaining long-term living is an instinctive desire to get in out of the rain.

The Indoorsman way of life is an equal and opposite reflection of the weather. If it is cold outside, the Indoorsman works to make the indoor space warm. If it is wet outside, the Indoorsman works to make the indoor space dry. If it is windy outside, the Indoorsman really does nothing differently to the indoor space, although there are certain kinds of wind that break indoors, but that's another danger altogether.

The point here is that constructing and accessorizing an indoor space that is inversely proportionate to the weather outside is the core value of the Indoorsman way of living. Does he consider the weather to be dangerous? Yes. But this does not indicate that he is running from this danger in a state of fear. On the contrary, he is not running from the weather; he is conquering the weather, counterbalancing its fierce and relentless attack with his own fierce and relentless pursuit of safety and comfort.

Indeed, being free to live well indoors, despite the weather outdoors, is the essence of the chief narrative of humanity itself. It's the story of us.

6. THE SUN AND SUNBURNS

As has already been stated, unpredictable weather is the most imminent outdoor danger. But another variable also presents innumerable challenges—and this particular one is not at all unpredictable. The presence of the sun is a constant in the outdoors, and it shouldn't be taken lightly.

The sun is both a blessing and a curse to all who venture outdoors beneath its blazing fury. To those lost at night and wandering through dangerous terrains where wild, nocturnal creatures are tracking their every move, the emergence of the sunrise over the horizon is nothing less than a beacon of hope. These early rays of light illuminate the landscape and allow travelers to continue forward on sure footing.

Even though the sun is an outdoor feature, one cannot deny that it is truly a marvel. A star composed of plasma and combustible gases ablaze at 27 million degrees Fahrenheit and located some 93 million miles away from earth, the sun somehow perfectly warms and illuminates the earth, allowing animals and plants to grow and thrive.

Even so, the sun can be dangerous, as any Indoorsman knows. If a person spending time away from the indoors experiences prolonged exposure to the sun's harmful ultraviolet rays, they can suffer from headaches, heat rashes, nausea, heatstroke, and even death. But even if someone spends too much time in the sun, yet through hydration and other proven health techniques finds a way to avoid these most detrimental consequences, they can still experience sunburn.

Sunburn is an Indoorsman's worst outdoor nightmare—other than being trampled to death by a herd of angry wildebeests or living in one of those Scottish castles in which the Loch Ness Monster can fit during a loch dam breach. But the fact remains that Indoorsmen are much more susceptible to sunburn because their skin

generally doesn't experience as much daily exposure to the sun as non-Indoorsmen. Normal exposure to the sun allows the skin's pigment to darken in slow, manageable stages. Some call this darkened skin a tan. In rare cases, Indoorsmen have been known to achieve what can be called a mild tan, but it rarely lasts more than a few weeks because they almost instinctively head back to the safety of their indoor lair.

Sudden exposure to the sun can be devastating to the Indoorsman's delicate melatonin equilibrium, and things can escalate very quickly. In fact, a pasty Indoorsman can suffer significant levels of sunburn in less than an hour of exposure to direct sunlight, especially in equatorial or high-elevation areas where the sun is closer to the earth.

Just as color-coded emergency awareness systems in hospitals and secret military facilities monitor the global movements of aggressive national adversaries, generally reserving the color red for the direst of situations, the Indoorsman meets his greatest risk when his skin transitions from white to red. The following Emergency Sunburn Awareness System is especially helpful for those moments when Indoorsmen are traveling in groups. This way, when one notices another's skin is experiencing movement on the scale, he can simply call out the following codes.

INDOORSMAN'S EMERGENCY SUNBURN AWARENESS SYSTEM

- Code White: All is well. The Indoorsman's skin still resembles that of a newborn baby.

- Code Tan: Generally reserved for non-Indoorsmen; that is, humans who can actually achieve a tan.

- Code Pink: Exercise caution. Epidermal reddening (also known as sunburning) appears to have begun in small stages.

- Code Orange: Evaluate escape options. Either the skin is approaching a sunburn or the Indoorsman recently received a spray tan.

- Code Red: Seek shelter immediately. Face, arms, and shoulders are visibly sunburned.

One final note here: While all sunburns are dangerous to the Indoorsman, no pain can compare with a sunburn of the tops of one's feet. One would assume that other areas, such as the abdomen, chest, or face, would be more painful, and they certainly carry their own levels of discomfort. But to the Indoorsman, a burning of the top of his feet can incapacitate him for days on end. The burn itself is similar in pain to sunburns on other parts of the body, but the fact that the feet have to bend and move to walk to the restroom means that each step becomes mandatory and excruciating. And if the Indoorsman is forced to go outside for some reason, putting on any type of shoes is its own form of torture.

So, as an Indoorsmen, if you have no choice but to be exposed to the danger of the sun, wear sunscreen, a hat, sunglasses, and clothes that completely cover every part of your body in such a way that will still permit you to be able to walk. But above all else, be sure your feet are completely covered. Flip-flops and sandals may not do the trick, as your feet can still be burned, although you will have striking grill marks on your feet from the sandal straps.

When one is forced to be outside, the truest Indoorsman technique is to simply put on socks with one's flip-flops or sandals. While socially unacceptable to the outside world, socks and sandals offer the Indoorsman a shame-free level of comfort, safety, and style. Wear them with the pride and dignity that come with being an Avid Indoorsman in the modern world.

7. QUICKSAND

While it is impossible to list all of the dangers the outdoors presents, no one can refute that quicksand is one of the greatest threats. Sure, it can be argued that one rarely encounters quicksand in the out-of-doors, but such an argument obviously comes from an Outdoorsman and not an Indoorsman, because only by being outside could such a conclusion be made.

Therefore, Indoorsmen are prone to consider almost all outdoor threats as equal and imminent. Besides, a favorite movie of Indoorsmen around the world, *The Princess Bride*, proves that quicksand can indeed be quick—and deadly. In the scene where Westley and Buttercup must traverse the dangerous fire swamp, Buttercup takes a step onto what appears to be merely a sandy area of the forest. Suddenly she falls completely into the quicksand hole, which closes up above her, sealing her fate. It is only after Westley cuts a nearby vine and courageously dives headfirst into the quicksand to retrieve her that hope emerges from the depths of the quicksand.

This could definitely happen to you.

Yes, true Indoorsmen recognize the difference between fiction and reality, except perhaps in regard to reality television. Regardless, there is an awareness that quicksand may not instantly suck an individual downward as it did in *The Princess Bride*. However, it is likely that it will.

Or perhaps your demise from quicksand will be a much slower process. Therefore, if you ever find yourself slowly sinking in quicksand, it is best to scream as loudly and hysterically as you can, using up all your strength and hopefully falling into an unconscious state very quickly. This way, your body will go limp and motionless, which will slow your descent into the quicksand and certain death.

Or you could just reach for a nearby branch or a rope and pull yourself to safety. Either method is effective.

ESTABLISHING A HEALTHY INDOORS ROUTINE

Good health and good sense are two of
life's greatest [indoor] blessings.

PUBLILIUS SYRUS

Many stereotypes about the Indoorsman way of life must be addressed so they can either be confirmed or denied. One such stereotype is that Indoorsmen are unhealthy due to a sedentary lifestyle, erratic sleeping patterns, and poor dietary choices. Therefore, it would be helpful to both evaluate and educate those interested in learning about Indoorsmanship concerning what it means to seek a healthy lifestyle within this particular philosophical paradigm.

Before we get to the specifics, let's begin by defining healthy. In our day, health is often tied to a particular expectation of one's physical appearance. We tend to think that being healthy means maintaining a healthy weight or being able to achieve sustained levels of physical and cardio activity.

Many people pursue strength training as the ultimate expression of a healthy lifestyle. CrossFit and other modern exercise programs have seen their gyms (or boxes, as they are called in CrossFit) literally flooded (well, not really "literally" flooded, as in the sense of a literal flooding of water) with people from all walks of life, including those of a more natural athletic persuasion as well as those who don't really fit the bill but are more than willing to spend many bills for permission to lift dangerously heavy weights together.

It seems that everyone from former Marines to soccer moms to former Marine soccer moms (and others too) have joined the national phenomenon that seems to be producing a sense of unbridled joy, except, obviously, in the cases where Cross-Fitters are required to wear heavy bridles as a part of their routine. Then it can best be described as "bridled joy." Either way, these athletes engage in interval training techniques of lifting free weights as a form of extreme cardio, all the while joining in with the onlooking community who produce raucous shouts of encouragement and challenge that can best be described as "a collectively happy exercise rage riot."

CrossFit is like Jazzercise meets *Braveheart* meets a Dr. Phil marathon meets an actual marathon.

But for the Indoorsman, the pursuit of health simply begins with establishing a routine. This routine may differ in various ways from conventional health and fitness regimens, but it is no less effective—depending on how you measure effectiveness, which might render it slightly less effective.

1. THE HEALTHY ROUTINE OF SLEEP

The Avid Indoorsman values sleep above almost every other aspect of his health plan. In fact, he has been known to randomly pause other activities, such as exercising or eating, to engage in sleep. That's how important it is to him, and rightly so. The following are some key components of his healthy sleep routine.

A. Hours of Sleep

Researchers have concluded that those who do not get an appropriate amount of sleep have much shorter life spans, are more likely to die from anything at any time, gain more weight, become more forgetful, appear to be older than they actually are, and become sick more often than those who experience the appropriate amount of sleep. In fact, those who average less than five hours of sleep per night actually double their risk of dying from cardiovascular disease, which is the number one cause of death in the United States.

Indoorsman research has found that, as much as sleep deprivation can harm one's overall health, the practice of Sleep Superfluity can inversely enhance one's health. Adding more sleep in excessive amounts to one's daily routine can actually improve the quality and length of one's life. This is one of the main reasons people are migrating in droves to the Indoorsman lifestyle. The following chart reveals the intriguing and exciting possibilities that sleep produces for an Indoorsman's lifespan.

INDOORSMAN THEORY OF SLEEP SUPERFLUITY

	Number of Hours of Sleep per Night (or Day)	Average Lifespan
Unhealthy Non-Indoorsman	4 hours	45 years
	4.5 hours	50 years
	5 hours	55 years
	5.5 hours	60 years
	6 hours	65 years
Healthy Indoorsman	7 hours	75 years
	9 hours	85 years
	11 hours	95 years
	13 hours	105 years
	15 hours	115 years

As this scientific research attests, Avid Indoorsmen can virtually guarantee themselves a lifespan of 115 years simply by disciplining themselves to sleep 15 hours every day or night. To the non-Indoorsman, this may just appear to be laziness or lethargy—and exercised (so to speak) outside of certified Indoorsman research, methodology, and oversight, that is indeed what it can become. But when integrated into a holistic Indoorsman lifestyle, Sleep Superfluity can drastically enrich your life, even though you will not be awake as much to realize it.

B. Most Common Sleep Deterrents

While chasing after more sleep should be one of your life's pursuits, you should still expect challenges along the way, mainly from the fact that your family, friends, bosses, and spouse may not understand or accept your desire to live well into your hundreds. Buying a copy of this book for them may help, but other than the relational hiccups that occur from excessive sleeping, the greatest practical pitfalls to a good night's rest for the Indoorsman are:

- Dinging phone notifications from your various social media feeds

- Binge-watching a show and succumbing to the temptation to start just one more episode instead of going to bed

- The ambient and LED light emitted from all the devices in the room

- Insomnia initiated by worry that an approved automatic overnight OS update will malfunction and render your phone frozen in the morning, which will also disable your alarm and make you late for work

- A long text thread with a friend—a conversation that probably could have been completed on the phone in less than three minutes

- Insomnia caused by the excitement of waiting for a large .mov or .wav file to finish rendering after you have worked on it all day, and you just can't wait to experience the final product (and possibly upload it to social media)

- A malfunctioning Clapper that keeps mistaking the gurgling sound of your snoring as a signal to turn on the lights

- The disturbing Darth Vader sound of your sleep apnea (CPAP) machine

C. Choosing a Mattress

While there are numerous other topics related to an Indoorsman's sleep, none may be more important than the actual surface upon which you rest—your mattress and pillows. Choosing the right mattress is no simple task, and it is not a choice to be made quickly or taken lightly.

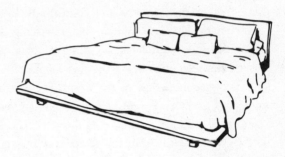

Perhaps this is why the mattress business is a billion-dollar industry. Even in smaller towns, there can be upward of five to seven mattress stores under construction at any given time. It is rare to see more than two people per week actually enter a mattress store, so their ability to stay open or actually make a profit remains something of a mystery—except for the fact that mattresses are now so expensive that simply selling one or two mattresses per year seems to be sufficient to keep an entire store comfortably afloat from a financial standpoint.

Yes, mattresses are expensive, but that does not mean you should necessarily go hunting for deals outside of the conventional mattress industry. There is a certain cultural dialogue going around these days about what happens to a mattress after owning it for several years—and the news isn't pleasant. In fact, one popular mattress company advertised the following information in their store: "After eight years, an old mattress becomes a heavy weight from pounds of dead skin, gallons of sweat, and millions of dust mites that accumulate inside it!"

The obvious solution is to leverage your house or possibly one of your kidneys in order to finance the purchase of a high-priced mattresses—and to do so every eight years, by the way. (Obviously, from a physical standpoint, you can probably only leverage one kidney in your lifetime.)

Unless you are a microbiologist with your own lab and testing supplies, it's almost impossible to know if the gruesome description these mattress stores provide about the innards of mattresses is really describing the inside of *your* mattress. Perhaps it is and perhaps it's not, but the real question for the Avid Indoorsman is: Are all of those millions of skin cells and dust mites making the mattress more or less comfortable for sleeping?

Yes, comfort is key when it comes to the Indoorsman's sleep patterns. Obviously, each person's body is uniquely shaped, reacting differently to various levels of softness and firmness, so there is no definitive way to proclaim one particular level of mattress softness or firmness as the obvious choice for all Indoorsmen. But you can pretty much guarantee that the Indoorsman's choice will be significantly softer than that of his Outdoorsman counterpart, who may very well sleep on the forest floor with nothing but sticks, stones, and other bone-breaking debris as his makeshift mattress.

No wonder he claims that words will never hurt him—he's too worried about his aching back to listen.

But for the Indoorsman, there are a variety of choices for mattresses. The first suggestion when shopping for a mattress is to be bold—lie upon each and every bed in the store for as long as you want and do your best to mimic most of the things that happen in your bed at home. Roll over on different sides. Get under the sheets. If the bed doesn't have sheets, bring some from home. Have your spouse or child hold up a small television or tablet while you watch an entire episode of your favorite show (even a rerun, if necessary) from the mattress store bed. Bring a few snacks and drinks, taking note of how easily the crumbs sweep off the mattress. Also, it may be helpful to bring your CPAP or sound machine from home as well. Consider it your own informal sleep study.

Let your kids run amok through the store, jumping on each and every mattress, just as they would at your house—especially if your house contains a mattress showroom inside. How else are you to decide unless you re-create the realities of your indoor domain in the mattress store? Yes, it may make the salespeople a bit uncomfortable, but remind them that this experience is actually about your comfort, not theirs. In other words, no matter what firmness of mattress you choose, be firm in the process of choosing it.

After all, you'll still be making payments on this mattress long after its insides have been replaced with dead skin cells and dust mites, so you have to get this decision right.

2. THE HEALTHY ROUTINE OF EXERCISE

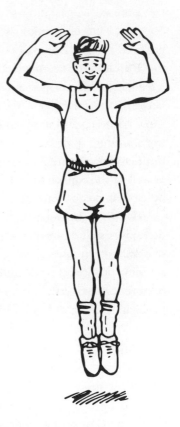

Exercise is another key area in the Indoorsman's life in which stereotypes abound. There are those who say that the Indoorsman is stationary, stiff, and sedentary. But these are misrepresentations of the lowest sort. The Avid Indoorsman can actually be a pristine picture of fitness—even if that picture requires some filters or cropping.

A. Philosophy

The chief philosophical slant regarding exercise for the Indoorsman is that one may exercise anyway he or she pleases, especially considering the abundance of indoor fitness opportunities available, such as running on a treadmill, riding a stationary bike, doing yoga, lifting weights, and performing P90X and insanity.[1] Surprisingly, it is also not uncommon or inappropriate for Indoorsmen to venture into the outdoors for short stints of exercise. In fact, many Indoorsmen have been known to be proficient runners, cyclists, kayakers, and driveway

---

1. There is also a series of exercise videos called Insanity that have proven to be effective as well.

basketball players. But, as always, these outside activities represent intentional and temporary exits from one's indoor domain.

B. Standing Up Occasionally

So, then, these isolated activities notwith-standing, any Indoorsman can still find plenty of other unconventional ways to exercise without leaving the confines of his or her indoor space. In general, a good rule of thumb (not to be confused with thumb-strengthening exercises for texting or tweeting) is to make sure you get up from your laptop or couch (or both) to move around the room at least once or twice a day. Some Indoorsmen attempt this exercise between commercials or as the next episode of a show is loading during a Netflix binge. Regard-less of the timing, this technique will ensure that an adequate amount of blood continues to flow throughout your limbs and extremities, and, hopefully, your brain as well. If you happen to be at a desk, this will also ensure that the wheels of your office chair do not make permanent indentations in your carpet.

Many Avid Indoorsmen have engaged in the growing trend of using standing desks. Research shows that standing rather than sitting can decrease your chances of obesity, heart disease, cancer, diabetes, and early death. Who knew, right? So a standing desk could be helpful in furthering your health and fitness—and it also diminishes the excessive time and energy required to actually get up from your chair to get another donut from the kitchen.

C. Finger Circuit Training

Button-pushing exercises are extremely helpful for muscle development, spe-cifically in the finger muscle groups. One can improve finger strength, speed, and dexterity by engaging in an intentional training circuit of pushing the buttons on the remote control or even the digital buttons on their phone or tablet. It is impor-tant to note that the resistance level is highly varied between actual and digital

buttons, so it may be helpful to time yourself on each device, but only after you've built up your stamina to a safe button tolerance. These kinds of exercises will really help you train for television or movie marathons.

D. Other Miscellaneous Exercises and the Modem Plank

Other Indoorsman exercise techniques include periodic popping of your knuckles and toes, slowly rubbing your hands through your hair while letting out a long sigh, searching through your smallest kitchen drawers for extra AA batteries that will fit your Bluetooth mouse or keyboard that has been performing sluggishly as of late, mining the deep and infinite recesses of your Swiss Army backpack for a missing receipt, and leaning over to unplug your modem and holding this position for 30 seconds as it resets. This exercise is actually called the modem plank.

After consulting your doctor before engaging in any of these exercises, you should also be sure to practice proper stretching techniques to avoid muscle and brain cramping. Or simply purchasing stretchy pants will probably do the trick.

3. THE HEALTHY ROUTINE OF EATING

It is said that some people eat to live while other people live to eat. So which statement is most true for the Avid Indoorsman?

The answer is simply "yes," as the following perspectives explore.

A. Perceptions and Realities

While the research is still ongoing, it is a fairly certain fact that people require food in order to survive, which probably explains the widespread historical success of grocery stores, restaurants, Amazon food delivery, and lunch box companies. It would appear that the act of eating isn't going away anytime soon.

As we have learned so far, the Indoorsman mind-set differs from the conventional or outdoor mind-set on most everything imaginable. This is no different when it comes to food and food choices. As they do in many other facets of life, stereotypes abound in this area of Indoorsman living. These gross assumptions about the eating habits and the resulting physical and psychological effects upon the Indoorsman's physique and energy levels are rarely accurate, mainly because the source of their research is nothing more than popular observation occasionally mixed with medical science.

But perceptions do not necessarily equate to reality, as is demonstrated by the following chart. And, of course, no one body type, weight, or appearance defines all Indoorsmen; that is, they come in all shapes and sizes.

PERCEPTIONS VS. REALITIES OF APPEARANCES RESULTING FROM INDOORSMAN EATING HABITS

1. **The Indoorsman Appears to Be** *Frail*

    Perception: His diet renders him unable to sustain extended physical activity.

    Reality: He never gets asked to help his friends when they move.

2. **The Indoorsman Appears to Be** *Skinny*

    Perception: His diet keeps him from getting the right amount of proteins and nutrients.

    Reality: His butt fits in his kid's car seat, allowing him a surprisingly comfortable and much safer ride on highways.

3. **The Indoorsman Appears to Be** *Flabby*

    Perception: His diet renders him incapable of completing Navy SEAL training.

    Reality: He has actually sculpted his body to be his own flotation device.

4. **The Indoorsman Appears to Be** *Lethargic*

    Perception: His diet makes him so weak that he gets winded walking up a single flight of stairs.

    Reality: He actually avoids stairwells due to the probable loss of cellular signal.

5. **The Indoorsman Appears to Be** *Disinterested*

    Perception: His diet produces low blood sugar, which makes him standoffish in social situations.

    Reality: He's actually just avoiding questions about fixing other people's computers.

B. Portion Control

Regardless of appearances and realities, the Avid Indoorsman does pursue a specific dietary plan in order to maintain his particular lifestyle. This lifestyle includes a lot of eating out at restaurants, which from a conventional dietary perspective is problematic and counterintuitive to health and fitness. These problems are the result of restaurant fare generally being high in calories, high in sodium, and ridiculously overproportioned—often two to three times larger than the size of what nutritionists would consider a healthy serving size.

But the Avid Indoorsman is anything but conventional, so he finds a way to thrive under these conditions, especially when you consider the many variations of what Indoorsmen may consider a healthy weight or activity level to be. Changing one's definition of health really opens up a lot of new and exciting options.

In terms of portion size, the Indoorsman has no problem ordering something conventional health-conscious people might consider too big. On the contrary, the Indoorsman feels the ordering of food is as much about economic efficiency as anything else. By ordering a large appetizer or entrée, even if he doesn't finish eating it

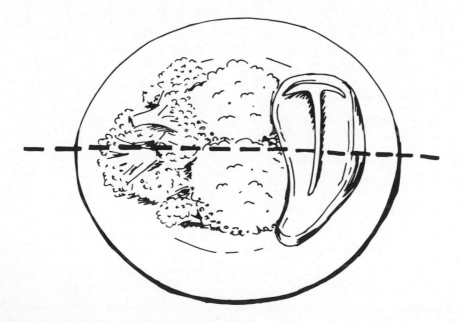

in one sitting, he can always take the rest home in a to-go box—or, as some call it, a doggie bag—to consume in place of another meal. Avid Indoorsmen may consume leftovers from doggie bags for more than 50 to 60 percent of their meals.

To be clear, no serious Indoorsman would ever feed his leftovers to his doggie—or even call his dog a doggie. Rather, he prides himself on building Styrofoam monuments to his miserly methods within his refrigerator, and each consumed leftover meal fondly reminds him of his recent restaurant experience and how that, like everything else, it is now being improved when it is brought into his indoor domain.

C. Domestic Indoor Radiation (Microwave)

To this end, some foods reheat better than others. While Outdoorsmen often pride themselves on cooking in the wild over a pit of coals or an open flame, Indoorsmen pride themselves on the ability to cook their food to a perfect consistency using nothing but government-regulated domestic levels of dangerous radiation.

While the microwave oven has been around since the 1960s, there is still no doubt the advent of this device is truly one of the most significant indoor advancements in history. It is an indoor miracle of sorts. Just consider that nothing but a flimsy plastic door separates the indoor chef from certain death Indiana Jones–style (i.e., the face-melting scene at the end of *Raiders of the Lost Ark*). Instead, the microwave connoisseur opens the magic door to retrieve a piping-hot meal fit for an indoor king.

Most Indoorsmen use the microwave much more than their other kitchen appliances—and often even in place of other household appliances. Besides the obvious popping of popcorn and reheating of three-day-old pizza, the microwave is often used to boil water, because who has time to wait for water to come to a boil on a stovetop? It is also good for melting butter or chocolate, either for direct consumption (butter shooters are an Indoorsman's guilty pleasure) or for use in a larger recipe. The microwave can also be used to iron out wrinkles in clothing simply by placing a damp shirt or undergarment inside and heating it to just below the melting point of the plastic buttons.

It is important to note that Indoorsmen who choose to use the microwave for uses or projects other than cooking food should adhere to a certain set of safety regulations. Above all, they should make sure there is no metal on anything they choose to zap with domestic radiation. While the microwave is safe, reliable, and fun to use for the whole family, if used incorrectly, it can quickly become a small nuclear device that will explode and possibly wipe out and contaminate your entire neighborhood block. Other than that, have a great time popping corn!

E. Indoorsman Nutritional Thought

Outside of leftovers and microwaving, there is a philosophical methodology to the Indoorsman's dietary reasoning. Although it has received much criticism in the modern age and has been disputed by many in the scholastic fields of medicine and nutrition, most people are at least somewhat familiar with the conventional food pyramid or some version of it. The food pyramid is a visual tool designed to help delineate and describe the best proportional balances of the various food groups in a seemingly healthy diet. Again, this pyramid is constantly changing as research continues to grow and new concepts continue to develop.

The Avid Indoorsman, being suspicious of pyramid schemes and often internalizing negative experiences from his or her high school trigonometry courses, does not subscribe to the conventional food pyramid unless it involves building an actual pyramid out of food for a historical Egyptian-themed party or event. Otherwise, a food pyramid creates too slippery of a slope (see previous entry on slippery slopes) for the Indoorsman's delicately refined palate and dietary philosophies.

Indoorsman dietary directives tend to trend less in the direction of triangles and more in the direction of circles. This is evident in the Indoorsman's body style. As the CrossFitter tends to be shaped like an upside triangle, the Indoorsman tends to be shaped like an upside-down circle.[2]

To this end, researchers have developed the Indoorsman Dietary Cycle (or IDC).[3] The best way to understand the IDC is to think of a laundry cycle. When doing laundry, certain combinations of clothing types and colors must be combined and separated in order to keep the wardrobe from shrinking, fading, or being dyed the wrong color. The same principles apply for the Indoorsman Dietary Cycle. The Indoorsman food groups break down into four categories: lights, darks, colors, and delicates.

The following breakdown gives examples of foods that fit into each of the IDC categories.

Indoorsman Dietary Cycle Food Type 1: Lights

Lights can generally be found on a menu under the heading of appetizers or possibly starters. Some people shorten the word *appetizers* to *apps*, but this can be confusing and irritating to the Avid Indoorsman, who does not want to mix terms when one definition, namely, apps that refer to computer or device applications, is already so crucial to his lifestyle. Thus, he will usually say the word *appetizers* instead.

Examples of appetizers include but are not limited to the following: chips and queso, chips and spinach dip (or spinach artichoke dip), cheese fries, nachos (with

---

2. Also known as a circle.

3. This has no direct correlation to the text abbreviation IDC, which means "I Don't Care," even though that is often how people assume Indoorsmen feel about their eating habits—and also perhaps how they often actually do feel.

just cheese), ultimate nachos (which may include sour cream, chives, jalapeños, guacamole, shredded beef, shredded chicken, etc.), onion rings, onion blossoms (not an actual blossom from an onion plant but rather the blossoming of a cooked onion caused by splaying it), cheese bites, and many more.

A special subset of appetizers are samplers, which are smaller portions of regular entrée menu items that are served as appetizers but without any of the sides that would normally accompany the entrée. These samplers can be singular or variable in their presentation. Examples of a single sampler are chicken tender samplers or slider samplers.[4]

Variable samplers are usually served with more than one item from the appetizer or entrée menu but in smaller portions. Variable samplers often use alliteration in their branding, such as Double Delights, Triple Teasers, or Quadruple Quesos. The possibilities are fairly endless in this category, as many restaurants offer a "create your own appetizer" menu from which customers can piece together their own variable sampler using their own combination of items from the restaurant's approved list.

Finally, one would be remiss to fail to mention that any breads (including rolls, biscuits, muffins, etc.) that are delivered to the table before the entrée fall into the lights category. This is also true of any salads or soups ordered to precede the main course.

Uppity Indoorsmen may also include in their lights category a charcuterie course, which, of course, is a tray of cheeses, each wrapped around a small piece of charcoal.[5]

For that matter, even uppityer Indoorsmen may opt for a single bite of sorbet that is served as a palate cleanser after the appetizer and before the darks (the entrée). Some nonuppity Indoorsmen have tried to adapt this sorbet practice for their own purposes by simply eating a medium-sized bowl of ice cream between their spinach dip, their barbecue ribs, and a second serving of ribs. Studies show this ice cream course doesn't do much in the way of palate cleansing, but it does taste good and leads to a fuller feeling than meals without it.

---

4. A slider is a small hamburger or cheeseburger and should not be confused with the pitch by the same name in baseball and hopefully not with any bodily symptoms one may experience after eating a slider.

5. Many people do not include charcoal in their charcuterie courses.

Indoorsman Dietary Cycle Food Type 2: Darks

Darks are a much larger food category than lights, as they are generally listed as entrées or main courses on restaurant menus. During the Renaissance, especially among the upper class, a great emphasis was placed on meals being served and consumed in distinct courses. But in the modern age, most people don't formally acknowledge these courses, tending to think of a meal as a single cohesive experience.

Thus, when the Indoorsman eats out at a restaurant, he is actually paying homage to time-honored traditions that have been practiced by Indoorsmen throughout history. Dating back to the ancient Greek Indoorsmen (Ανθρωποι εντός ο κτίριου, meaning "people within the indoors"), the dark course has always been considered the most important in terms of overall dietary health—or more accurately stated, happiness itself, which may or may not always encompass more conventional viewpoints of dietary health.

Entrées can include most anything imaginable, but they are mostly made up of popular food-related items that are edible. In general, these dishes use various sides and/or sauces to surround and accentuate a central and highlighted protein. These proteins are usually meats, but they can also be plant-based or artificially created substitutes, such as veggie burgers, tofu, tempeh, seitan, beans and legumes, jackfruit (yes, the tropical fruit, but it's meatlike consistency is surprisingly versatile), and huge seasoned and grilled portabella mushrooms that can successfully masquerade as meat patties. Of course, typical entrées that are built around a protein of some sort contain the classics: beef, chicken, shrimp, fish, pork, lamb, venison, bison, quail, shellfish, duck, Bigfoot, octopus, the occasional holiday parakeet, and so forth and so on.

The other components of dark food, of course, are the sides. It would really be impossible to list all the possibilities, but the most popular sides that accent a protein are roasted brussels sprouts, creamed spinach, mashed potatoes, French fries, asparagus, roasted new potatoes, sweet potato fries, loaded baked potatoes, loaded sweet potatoes, steamed broccoli, tomato-cucumber salad, and many more.

For many Avid Indoorsmen, sides can literally make the meal—or at least extend it past its recommended ending point. While conventional dietary experts unequivocally counsel against the superfluous consumption of extra food—a practice also known as snacking or grazing—the Indoorsman mind-set is instinctively hardwired for efficiency. This means that even after a meal is seemingly completed, the existence of extra sides, especially those left out on a counter or stovetop, provides opportunities for additional grazing to occur—purely in the name of efficiency, of course, so as not to needlessly waste anything that has been so arduously prepared and presented. In fact, this is the first part of Indoorsman philosophy of conservationism: Never let an extra side dish go uneaten.

Indoorsman Dietary Cycle Food Type 3: Colors

The food group category of colors is where the Indoorsman philosophies truly begin to diverge from the conventional path. This category is not based on a specific type of food or even a specific course in the meal. Rather, this is another expression of conservationism.

The colors food group consists of foods left uneaten on the plates of others, namely, relatives, close friends, and the occasional acquaintance (with certain caveats, of course). This group is labeled colors because it demonstrates the prismatic array of creative possibilities that exist within the Indoorsman Dietary Cycle, a veritable rainbow of culinary choices. Rather than merely describe another predictable food group, consider this another dimension of food thought: one man's discarded scraps is another man's treasure.

At first glance, the idea of eating off someone else's plate seems crude and disgusting, but nothing could be further from the truth. The Avid Indoorsman understands the fine line between dumpster diving and eating from the colors food group. For the most part, avoiding the former is a matter of sorting the colors properly, which means not just reaching for anything that you see on another person's plate.

Indoorsmen know that the best color food choices come from the unfinished plates of their children. Many treasures abound there in the form of extra, often untouched chicken nuggets, French fries, and the like. There must be an exercise of self-control here, or else you can cross a line and begin eating your children's food before they have actually had enough to eat. The possibility is understandable, considering the inconceivable snail's pace at which children seem to eat. Most Indoorsmen can finish several plates of food before their children can even take down half a cheeseburger. So, then, you must resist the urge to simply start taking food from their plates.

In general, your spouse will help you determine the moment you may start eating from the color menu. Listen for conversations with the children and statements such as, "Okay, honey. Yes, you've eaten enough. Just take your plate to the kitchen." At that point, it's "fare" game. Conversely, eye rolls from your spouse when you reach for the children's food are a dead giveaway that the time to do so has arrived; otherwise you will get a sound rebuke instead.

Regardless, when the time arrives, you must move quickly before your children unwittingly discard valuable food into the garbage. Though they are slow to eat, they can be quick to discard. It also helps to move with some discretion if, that is, you want to avoid any piercing stares of shame from any other adults in the room other than your spouse.

If the color you are about to eat is from the plate of your child or spouse, you can be free to eat at will; that is, eat the food any way you like, even if there are bites already missing. After all, you already share germs with these people. It will probably even help to galvanize your immune system through repeated overexposure to your family's unique bacteria.

But eating off a friend's plate is a different story. To avoid shame or ridicule, the friend must be someone with whom you are very close. This is not something to be done on a first date or ever at the table of your in-laws—unless you are invited by them to do so. If you have buddies with whom you golf, bowl, play in a band, or play cards or board games regularly, then you have definite color menu contributor candidates.

In general, it is appropriate to ask before reaching onto a nonbiological family member's plate, but the way you ask is of the utmost importance. This is a nuanced technique, so practice before you reach. You might say, "Hey, I've never ordered that dish here before." Wait and see if they offer you a taste. If they do not, you might venture a little further. "Do you mind if I sample that?"

Such a nonchalant approach will almost always produce good results, as if you are attempting to expand your already impressive culinary palate—which you are. But if you are asking about something that seems to be pedestrian, such as meat loaf or French fries, this approach can backfire. Again, above all else, you must not ask *too early* in the dining experience. There must be at least the appearance that they have finished or are near finishing their eating.

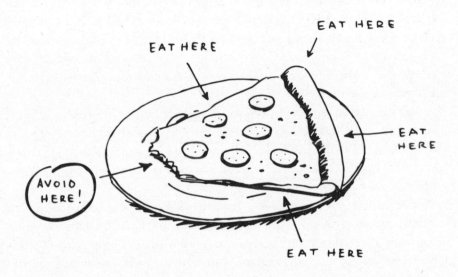

To this end, beware of slow chewers—those who seem to eat at the infuriating pace of children and the elderly. Some theorize their slow mastication is a purposeful attempt to draw the Indoorsman into a premature color food request. The veracity of such theories is, at best, suspect. But the point remains, if you find yourself waiting on a slow chewer, it is best to exercise self-control by putting their plate out of your mind and focusing on other color candidates at the table.

Finally, if approval has been given, the process of eating from nonfamily members' plates is simple—just do not bite directly from an area of the food from which they have already take a bite. This is impossible to do with food that is liquid or gelatinous in consistency, such as soup or pudding, so you'll have to make decisions regarding these kinds of foods as the details of your situation arise.

Again, be sure to eat around any places someone else's mouth has touched—unless, that is, they leave the table for any amount of time after they are obviously finished. Then, if you are comfortable with their current health and your own perceived level of immunity, you may eat their food at your leisure. If you do choose this path, eat quickly and try to remove the plate (or have a server clear the plate from the table) before the person from whose plate you have foraged returns. This way they will never suspect you may have eaten anything their mouth has also touched, assuming instead that you (or the server) have simply been courteous in cleaning up the table area.

Indoorsman Dietary Cycle Food Type 4: Delicates

The final category of the IDC is simply called the delicates. Non-Indoorsmen generally think of these foods as desserts, but to the Indoorsman they are indeed delicate and should be reverenced as such. Tragically, conventional food triangles do not include desserts. Furthermore, traditional food courses generally include them only at the end of a meal.

But for the IDC, much like the laundry cycle, delicates can and indeed should exist on their own merit; that is, they need not always be mixed in with the other courses. Thus, the Avid Indoorsman may partake of desserts with or without other parts of the meal. Cakes, ice cream, candies, frozen yogurt (also commonly referred to as FroYo among many Indoorsman types, especially of the hipster persuasion), and the like should always be strategically positioned throughout one's indoor space for the purpose of easy access to quick bursts of sugary sweet energy.

E. The Indoorsman Dietary Cycle at Work

Now that you understand the basics of the IDC, you may initiate your own cycle. If you use the laundry cycle concept, you will be tempted to separate lights, darks, colors, and delicates. But the true Avid Indoorsman knows—especially when one's spouse is away—that all clothes can be washed at once as long they are done so in cold water.

The same is true of this philosophy of eating. Eat as *you see fit*. (This is not to be confused with eating in a way that will make other people *see you as fit*.) Just be sure to utilize the simple guidelines you've learned in this study. And if you choose to combine all of the four food types into one meal, be sure to drink something cold to wash it all down. As in a laundry cycle, cold makes all of the IDC food groups mix together without fading or shrinking.

In fact, no Indoorsman has ever physically shrunk at all while using these simple eating philosophies and techniques. But many have found the act of eating much more satisfying and fulfilling.

F. The Art of Snacking

Finally, it should be noted that the Indoorsman's eating habits revolve as much around convenience as they do health. Ancient hunter-gatherer Indoorsmen foraged for berries, nuts, and honey so they could take them back to their caves or tents to consume with their families. These basic food components were the earliest form of snacks.

The modern Indoorsman honors this ancient cultural legacy by also engaging in a lifestyle that seeks after snacks. In fact, these same historical snacks of the ancient Indoorsmen can still be found in the culinary regimen of their modern descendants. Nuts, berries, and honey make up almost every granola-type snack available through Amazon food delivery.

There is a reason the Indoorsman is slanted toward snacking, and once again, it has to do with speed and efficiency. A quick snack can be grabbed during a commercial break so the viewer can quickly return to the show, having skipped the annoyances of the commercials. Yes, any serious Indoorsman will have access to DVR technology, which will allow him or her to fast-forward and/or pause, but there is still a principle of time and energy management here. Streaming services often require viewers to watch marketing ads. Either way, Indoorsmen do not like to spend too much time away from a particular show while looking for food because it breaks their flow of tracking whatever particular plot line, home remodel, or reality drama they are viewing.

Contrary to popular belief, the act of snacking is more of a responsibility than a privilege. Traditional snacks are infamous for the crumbs they can produce. These crumbs, if stewarded irresponsibly, can be deposited beneath and/or behind one's couch cushions, inviting unwanted visitors of a rodent or insect persuasion into one's indoor sanctuary.

This simply won't do. In order to avoid such an indoor fail, following are a few snack ideas that will help Novice Indoorsmen navigate their snacking successfully. Obviously, once one has ascended to a higher level of mastery, they may snack at their own leisure because they are fully equipped for proper crumb management. There are multiple options, but beginners may want to try the following three snacks in order to avoid or minimize crumb-based crises.

TOP THREE SNACKS FOR AVOIDING CRUMBS

1. *Pizza Rolls.* Quite possibly the most significant oven-driven snack ever created, these tiny bites of Italian delight are perfect for safe couch snacking. The best practice is to wait for them to cool, because fresh out of oven, they can reach temperatures hotter than the surface of the sun. But if you wait a few minutes, you can then pop them in your mouth one at a time. Otherwise, by taking smaller bites out of your pizza rolls, you risk the danger of dripping marinara sauce on your couch.

2. *Grapes.* If they could see you on your couch with a handful of grapes, your hunter-gatherer ancestors would paint a strangely futuristic cave drawing in your honor. Grapes are a great idea because they come naturally prepackaged for snacking. You may want to completely pluck each of them from their vine before bringing them to the couch, though. Otherwise, the tiny end pieces of the vine can remain attached to the grape and drop into the couch cushions like crumbs, which would defeat our purpose. But vine-free grapes are the perfect couch-friendly snack.

3. *Marshmallows.* Marshmallows are nothing less than a modern marvel of advanced civilization. If grapes afford the Indoorsman a natural snacking opportunity, marshmallows balance one's snacking equilibrium with something completely and utterly artificial to its very core.[6] Squishy, fluffy, sticky, edible, jet-puffed globs of pure white sugar may *fly in the face* of everything today's nutritionists warn us about concerning health and fitness, but on the couch, these little beauties may *fly into the mouth* of the Indoorsman by the bagful with nary a crumb being discarded upon one's living room furniture.

---

6. It is difficult to find the actual core of a marshmallow without proper lab equipment.

4. THE HEALTHY ROUTINE
OF DRINKING COFFEE

Perhaps no other single commodity more purely reflects the essence of the Indoorsman life than coffee. As much as space shuttles are powered by oxygen and hydrogen, the Indoorsman is powered by coffee.[7]

A. A Semi-Brief Brief on the History of Coffee

Coffee has an extremely rich Indoorsman heritage, but it actually dates back to ancient coffee forests on the Ethiopian plateau. Early legends attest that sometime well before the fourteenth century, a goat herder named Kaldi discovered coffee after he noticed his goats, after eating from a certain tree, became so energetic they would not sleep at night.

As with all things of value, the first thing Kaldi did was to bring this magic bean indoors and share his experience with an abbot at his local monastery. The abbot explored the matter further, concocting a drink that surprisingly kept him wide awake throughout the long hours of evening prayer. Soon all the monks at the monastery were ranting and raving about these energizing beans—except, of course, those who had recently taken vows of silence. Yet even their miming became much more spirited, so to speak.

It didn't take long for coffee to awaken the rest of world as the growing reputation of this bean that could produce such a beautiful elixir moved eastward, beginning with the Arabian Peninsula and eventually reaching to Persia, Egypt, Syria, and Turkey by the sixteenth century. From the beginning, coffee drinking was an Indoorsman experience, as it was enjoyed not only in homes but also in the many public coffeehouses (known as *qahveh khaneh*), which began to appear in cities across the Near East. These coffeehouses began springing up everywhere as all people from all walks of life saw the value of coming indoors together to share caffeine and conversation.

By the seventeenth century coffee had made its way to Europe, but some there found its seemingly mystical qualities simply too fantastic to be trusted, even ascribing it the dubious label "the bitter invention of Satan." In fact, in 1615 clergymen

---

7. Any descriptions regarding the proper functioning of a space shuttle may or may not be accurate, so do your own due diligence before joining a space program.

in Venice officially condemned coffee. Perhaps this is the where term "Dark Ages" first originated. If not, it certainly should have. The debate became so contentious that Pope Clement VIII was made aware of the matter. After tasting the beverage for himself and finding it to be obviously divine, he lifted the senseless clerical censure and lent coffee his universal endorsement.

Coffee was well on its way, which helped to form the modern indoors as we know it. Coffeehouses quickly became centers of social activity and communication in the major cities of England, Austria, France, Germany, and Holland. Oddly enough, coffee began to displace the common breakfast drinks of the time, which were wine and beer. People began starting their days with shots of caffeine instead of shots of alcohol, which made them feel surprisingly more awake and well prepared for the day. As a result, the overall quality of their work began to improve.

Not to be histrionic about this, but coffee literally saved civilization as we know it.

But even as coffee was establishing the very course of modern civilization in Europe, in the American colonies, tea somehow still managed to remain the favored drink of choice. This trend continued until 1773, when patriots rebelled against an unbearable tax on tea inflicted on them by King George III. The Boston Tea Party forever slanted the American mind away from tea toward coffee. This led Thomas Jefferson to proclaim coffee "the favorite drink of the civilized world."

Jefferson's Caffeination Proclamation, as it should have been known, served as a philosophical pillar of developing cultural thought in the eighteenth and early nineteenth centuries. However, as far as modern history is concerned, it has since been lost to the annals of time, eclipsed by other seemingly more significant writings and actions from Jefferson such as the Declaration of Independence and the Louisiana Purchase.

But no one can dispute Jefferson's accuracy concerning coffee, as many new nations laid their foundations on economies dependent on the coffee trade. Even before the turn of the nineteenth century, coffee had risen to prominence as one of the most profitable export crops in the world. In fact, to this day, coffee remains the most sought-after commodity in the world, second only to crude oil—but in certain more rugged indoor environments, such as hospitals and teachers' lounges, coffee and crude oil are often indistinguishable.[8]

---

8. All historical ascertainments pertaining to coffee and its saving of the world are adapted from information published by the National Coffee Association (NCA), http://www.ncausa.org/About-Coffee/History-of-Coffee.

B. Brewing Techniques

Just as apparently there is more than one known way to skin a cat, there is also more than a single way to brew a vat of this most essential of Indoorsman necessities. The true Avid Indoorsman will familiarize himself not only with his favorite coffee brewing method but will also be well rounded in the knowledge and skill of all brewing techniques so he will be fully equipped to have an intelligent coffee conversation, confidently order various kinds of coffee at meetings or visits at unfamiliar coffeehouses, and, most importantly, prepare coffee to the desired taste of his indoor guests.

Brewing Technique 1: Standard Drip Coffee

The historically most-used method for brewing coffee, the standard drip process, involves pouring water over ground coffee beans in an automatic machine. More traditional Indoorsmen may prefer their old Mr. Coffee pots because the method is easy, time tested, and produces a predictable quality of coffee.[9]

Brewing Technique 2: Chemex

Chemex sounds like a top-secret government-developed biological agent, but it is actually delightful. Ironically, it was originally developed around the same time as the atomic bomb in the 1940s, but no direct correlation has ever been made between the two. Similar to a standard drip machine, the Chemex machine also pours hot water over coffee grounds, but it keeps this water at a steady temperature of 180° to 200°. Thus, the Chemex machine requires a filter that is significantly thicker, resulting in a smoother texture and flavor.

---

9. In some academic circles, the correct term to avoid offense is "Dr. Coffee."

Brewing Technique 3: French Press

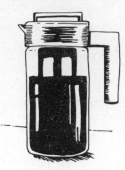

The French press method of preparing coffee is a lot like what would happen if a *French fry* method of eating potatoes had a baby with a *bench press* method of lifting weights. The result is delicious strength. The French press pitcher allows the Indoorsman to choose his or her strength of coffee and thus choose the level of caffeine in their coffee.

Brewing Technique 4: Cold Brew

Cold brewing is similar to the French press, except that it's almost completely opposite. It uses cold water instead of hot. Other than that, they are very much the same. The other difference between the two is the steeping time, which can be up to 12 hours for cold brew. Again, there are many similarities in their differences.

Brewing Technique 5: Instant Coffee

The very sound of this method of coffee production would seemingly be exactly what the Avid Indoorsman is searching for, but exercise caution here. Instant coffee is just that—instant. Simply by mixing a spoonful of ground coffee powder in hot water, you're ready to go in seconds. But you may notice a significant difference in taste and consistency from other more conventional coffee-brewing methods, mainly because instant coffee isn't technically coffee but rather a coffee extract that has been freeze-dried.

Brewing Technique 6: Single-Serve Coffee

The advent of the single-serve coffee craze is a testament to the brilliant efficiency of the Indoorsman mind-set. After all, who has three to five minutes to wait for an *entire* pot of coffee to brew when you can use a disposable pod filled with grounds? Keurig, the name of the most popular single-serve company, is actually a Dutch word that, loosely translated, means "jittery podhead."

C. Quantity Control vs. Quality Control

To the Avid Indoorsman, asking, "How much coffee is too much?" is like asking the Outdoorsman, "How many fish do you want to catch today?" There is no limit—except in fishing tournaments, where there is quite literally a limit.

There are societal stereotypes about coffee only being wake-up juice for people in the morning, but most true Indoorsmen don't just drink coffee after sunrise. They treat coffee like a magical fountain to be frequented throughout the day and night. In other words, there is a lot more to coffee than just caffeine. In fact, there are more than one thousand natural compounds in coffee beans.

But there's more, literally much more.

During the roasting process, 300 compounds are newly created, many of which are strong antioxidants that have numerous health benefits. These can sharpen memory, reduce stress, increase athletic performance and endurance, stop headaches, improve cognitive functioning in older adults, and also lift one's mood. Coffee may also reduce the risk of type 2 diabetes, cirrhosis of the liver, Parkinson's disease, and several cancers, including liver and colon.[10]

In other words, one would be a fool not to drink a lot of coffee each and every day.

But there are some mild side effects to ingesting too much caffeine. So know when to say when. The following chart will help.

---

10. See https://www.webmd.com/diet/features/the-buzz-on-coffee#1.

COFFEE CONSUMPTION GUIDELINES

When You Experience…	This Is Probably Happening…	Coffee Will Help This Way
Morning grogginess	Your internal coffee level is low	Will wake you up
Midmorning blahs	First cup is wearing off	Will replenish coffee levels
Hunger between meals	You're probably hungry	Will deter appetite
Your boss is yelling at you	You're slacking off on the job	Will comfort you
Bad breath	It's probably coffee breath	Will make it worse
Cold weather	It's probably cold outside	Will warm your innards
Hot weather	The sun is probably hot	Will equalize your temp
Lunch meeting going long	Your friend is oversharing	Will help you be attentive
Extreme jitters	Caffeine has overtaken you	Will not help—try decaf

HOW TO DRESS AND ACT LIKE AN AVID INDOORSMAN

Fashion is about dressing according to what's fashionable.
Style is more about being yourself [indoors].

OSCAR DE LA RENTA

The Avid Outdoorsman may live in such a way that the *man* makes the clothes—perhaps out of flimsy sheets of tree bark woven together with thread composed of meticulously twisted timber fibers, along with dried, slitted, and splotchy accents. The Avid Indoorsman, however, lives in such a way that the *clothes* make the man.

As has been previously stated, no single attribute characterizes all Indoorsmen, and that truth applies here as well. There is no Indoorsman uniform; that is, one size does not necessarily fit all. But there are methodologies, trends, and boundaries that most Indoorsmen recognize when it comes to the way they dress.

The Indoorsman's clothing mantra is easy to remember: simple, sleek, and sweatpants.

1. SIMPLE

No other word encapsulates the clothing philosophy of the Indoorsman more than *simple*, which is why it is the first word in the aforementioned mantra. For many, simplicity is something to be avoided or disregarded. That is why words like *simpleton* are rarely used in a positive manner. Simply put, the world seems to exist in a constant state of increasing complication. But for the Indoorsman, it shan't be so. Before one can ever bring back sexy, he must bring back simple.

The wardrobe of the true Indoorsman can often be fit onto a single rack in his closet, which is helpful if he is sharing the closet with other less-simple people who like to fill endless hangers and shoe racks with an ever-growing collection of clothes for every occasion. For the Indoorsman, there are certainly occasions for which his choice of attire may change, but even so, the number of these occasions he prepares for pales in comparison to the clothes hound for whom no quantity of fabric and accessory is sufficient.

When learning to dress like an Indoorsman, begin with simplicity in mind. You will find that gray, black, and navy blue pretty much match everything, and thus they are also appropriate for almost every situation. Do not be surprised if there isn't someone in your life who desires that you would expand your design palate by wearing a greater variety of colors. This is a normal part of being an Indoorsman, and their suggestions should be received and evaluated respectfully.

In other words, don't arrogantly flaunt your sense of simplicity. In fact, you can expect certain people in your life (a spouse, a parent, or an in-law) to graciously purchase clothes to add to your wardrobe. When you open their gift, you will find yourself genuinely excited for the sentiment and deliberating over the possibility of widening your viewpoint. But don't be surprised when these gifts continue to accumulate in your closet next to the simple clothes your wear every day. Now, when certain events or holidays come around, you may want to branch out and wear one of these other colors in the presence of the one who gave you the gift, but otherwise the Indoorsman is always drawn to simplicity more than variety.

In that vein, the Indoorsman mind is almost instinctively programmed against a certain color palate: pastels. This particular group of hues and shades can actually make him emotionally and physically agitated. Again, there are times when he will think that wearing such colors might be possible, but rarely will he leave his indoor space wearing them. The only exceptions are Easter Sunday or when he is forced to be part of a friend's wedding—these are both instances in which non-Indoorsman types sense an opportunity to attempt to liberate the Indoorsman from his simplicity.

You may have to temporarily accommodate them, but you can expect to feel uncomfortable until the event is over and the pastels have returned to their permanent resting place—buried in a sea of hangers between the clothes you actually wear.

2. SLEEK

Simple may be the clothing philosophy of the Indoorsman, but sleek is the practical execution of it. Besides a basic color palate of gray, black, and navy blue, he will also choose fabrics that are durable, long-lasting, well-insulated against the elements, and above all else, comfortable.

Blue jeans are a staple of such a paradigm implementation because they represent both simplicity and practical use. Blue jeans were originally developed by Jacob W. Davis and Levi Strauss in the late nineteenth century for an especially rugged breed of Indoorsmen: miners. These men and women spent their days actually digging, chipping, and blasting new indoor spaces into the heart of hills and mountains.

Their pants of choice then initiated a global trend today, as Indoorsmen still prefer blue jeans when they venture into whatever mine their day calls for, whether that is a shift at a retail store or kiosk at the mall, an appointment at the Apple Store, a writing session at the local Starbucks, or an all-nighter at their homes while designing websites or trading Bitcoins from their laptops.

Blue jeans beautifully reflect the sleek versatility of the Indoorsman whose legs fill them. This is why some Indoorsmen have been known to wear the same pair of jeans every day for more than 15 years—now *that* is a good investment.

The other incredible attribute of blue jeans is

their rare ability to clean themselves. Self-cleaning ovens may be a modern marvel, but self-cleaning jeans have been around for more than a hundred years. Most of their cleaning power comes from their tendency to repel all manner of stains—or at least absorb and mask stains so they are difficult to see.

For these reasons, jeans rarely have to be washed. Some Indoorsman have been known to go several months wearing the same pair of jeans every day with no washing. But as demonstrated in the following chart, there is actually a moment when you will need to wash your jeans.

BLUE JEAN WASHING GUIDE

Your Jeans	This Is Probably Happening	So Do This
Feel super tight	You just washed them	Do lunges to stretch them
Feel somewhat snug	You washed them a few days ago	Wear them normally and wait
Feel perfect	You've entered the sweet jean spot	Whatever you do, don't wash them
Have a small stain	You were careless with the ketchup	Wear and scrub the spot with a damp cloth
Have a large stain	You have children	Take off and scrub the stain with a wet cloth
Smell slightly unpleasant	You've worn them for thirty days	A subtle spray of cologne
Smell very unpleasant	You've worn them for 60 days	Take off to air out for a day
Smell enough to elicit complaints	You've gone too far	Wash to reset natural cycle

3. SWEATPANTS

The final category described in the clothing mantra is the culmination of the entire matter. One should not make the mistake of thinking the sweatpants category only describes sweatpants themselves. Rather, sweatpants are a good description of the philosophical boundaries of comfort within which the Indoorsman seeks to live and dress.

This is where the Latin Indoorsman phrase *acta non verba* ("actions more than words") really comes into play. While there are guidelines, sweatpants encapsulate the bigger picture—the daily decisions the Indoorsman makes on the fly, which generally revolve around comfort.

Make no mistake. No respectable Indoorsman wears sweatpants in public unless he or she is going to work out, run, or paint a neighbor's house. But within the confines of his own indoor domain, sweatpants are a staple garment. They offer superior comfort as a result of their tendency to leave the lower body unencumbered yet still temperature regulated.

Sweatpants afford the Indoorsman the luxury of reclining in any position on any indoor piece of furniture, from the couch to the recliner (hence the name) to the occasional lazy day spent in bed. They are also helpful for performing chores around the house with full mobility as one squats, leans, reaches, and performs generally any physical activity.

The term *sweatpants* is actually a misnomer. Sweating does not always occur when one wears said pants. In fact, it is preferable if one does not sweat in their sweatpants as their fabric is not always as odoriferously forgiving as other Indoorsman apparel, such as blue jeans. Some have been known to cut off their sweatpants, converting them into sweatshorts. This is a fine practice, but it cannot be overemphasized that these can only be worn in the indoors or perhaps one's own yard.

The following chart will help you determine what manner of sweatpants work best for your current level of Indoorsmanship.

SWEATPANTS COMFORT SCALE

Predominant Fabric	Comfort Level (1 Being Lowest)	Downside
Cotton	4—Fairly comfortable	Shrinks after washing
Polyester	3—Moderately comfortable	Who wears polyester?
Jersey	2—Very comfortable	Holds no warmth
Fleece	1—Ultra comfortable	A true sweat pant

While the sweatpants category constitutes more of a bird's-eye view of the desire for comfort, there are actual components of sweatpants themselves that are related to functionality, mainly pockets and drawstrings.

SWEATPANTS STYLE GUIDE

1. *Situation:* Lying around the house all day with nowhere to go.

   a. Pro- or Anti-Drawstring?

   Anti-Drawstring. Drawstrings were developed with one purpose in mind: to keep one's pants from falling down unexpectedly. The lack of physical movement and activity eliminates the need for a drawstring in this scenario.

   b. Pro- or Anti-Pocket?

   Pro-Pocket. Unlike conventional pants, sweatpants pockets are not limited in purpose to carrying things as you move in the outside world. In this case, pockets can help you keep up with your phone or the remote control as you make trips to the kitchen for snacks and/or drinks.

2. *Situation:* Staying at home but cleaning the house.

    a. Pro- or Anti-Drawstring?

> *Pro-Drawstring.* Considering the main purpose of drawstrings, it only makes sense that when one is going to be running a vacuum, mopping, and cleaning bathroom mirrors, a drawstring is a solid choice. Otherwise, the amount of walking and reaching could cause a bad case of USS (undesired sweatpants saggage).

    b. Pro- or Anti-Pocket?

> *Anti-Pocket.* While cleaning the house, wearing sweatpants with pockets may not be the worst idea, as pockets could provide a place to carry one's phone, which will allow one to listen to podcasts or music via Bluetooth headphones while they clean. But the best practice is to leave the phone in a centralized location (within Bluetooth range) until the cleaning process is complete. This will allow one to periodically check notifications while avoiding extended moments of distraction during the cleaning process.

3. *Situation:* Running to Walmart or the grocery store.

    a. Pro- or Anti-Drawstring?

> *Pro-Drawstring.* For evidence of the unfortunate consequences of not choosing a pro-drawstring path in this scenario, one needs to look no further than their local Walmart, wherein many misguided shoppers break this rule and venture out without drawstrings. Sweatpants are nothing to be trifled with, and those who attempt public activity without drawstrings are tragic exhibits of the possible catastrophic results.

    b. Pro- or Anti-Pocket?

> *Pro-Pocket.* Again, the purpose of pockets in sweatpants is to carry small electronic devices as well as keys. So, then, it only

makes sense that one would choose pockets for a trip to the store.

4. *Situation:* Taking a long run or working out.

  a. Pro- or Anti-Drawstring?

  Pro-Drawstring. In cold weather climates, sweatpants can be a good choice, especially if one wears a type of sweatpants specifically designed for athletic activity. In such a case, the activity itself calls for the presence of a drawstring. There's nothing worse than losing your pants while you round the local park running trail.

  b. Pro- or Anti-Pocket?

  Anti-Pocket. This may be a surprise for many people, but if you are going to exercise, pockets can be problematic. The main reason is that their intended use—carrying devices or other small items—can hinder the run. If one runs with something small in their pocket, it can begin to generate its own centrifugal motion, rocking back and forth inside the pocket in sync with the motion of one's legs. It will appear that your pants are doing their own little dance as you run. Also, this is another reason for a drawstring as the inertia from the items in the pocket can cause sudden USS.

5. *Situation:* Riding in the car on a long road trip.

  a. Pro- or Anti-Drawstring?

  Anti-Drawstring. While a road trip will have moments of public interaction at gas stations and restaurants along the way, for all intents and purposes, it is the equivalent of lying around the house. The car is merely a portable indoor space, so you can treat it accordingly.

  b. Pro- or Anti-Pocket?

  Pro-Pocket. Unlike the act of exercising or working out, it is a good practice to have pockets in one's sweatpants during a car ride. The irony is that these pockets will probably not be used most of the time because one's keys will be in the ignition and one's phone will either be in one's lap or mounted on some third-party product attached to the windshield or a vent.

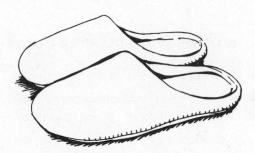

4. HONORABLE MENTIONABLES: SLIPPERS

Within the sweatpants category are many clothing-related topics of interest, but none is more important than footwear. While some Indoorsman historians claim the Vietnamese were wearing some type of slipper as early as the twelfth century, the actual English term *slipper* has its origin in Middle English dating back to sometime before the year AD 1000, when it was known as *sliper* or *slypescoh* in Middle and Old English respectively, the latter literally meaning "slip-shoe."

By the late fifteenth century, however, the term had evolved into the modern word *slipper*, which is a type of loose, light indoor footwear so named from the notion that it is a shoe that is slipped onto the foot. This etymology debunks the commonly held cultural opinion that a slipper keeps one from slipping on the floor.

To the modern Indoorsman, slippers can also refer to other types of footwear that he or she wears indoors, flip-flops, padded sandals, or even thinly crafted sneakers whose shoestrings are left loose for the purpose of quick slipping on and off. So, then, the negative stereotypes of someone wearing slippers do not always apply, because the Indoorsman's primary footwear of choice can have many variations.

But the purposes of indoor footwear remain the same, the most critical one being warmth. Nothing is more detrimental to a positive indoor experience than cold feet. Many Indoorsmen complain that their children or spouses place their extremely cold feet on their legs, causing them to scream or jerk away from these frigid family phalanges. To be clear, socks are often not sufficient to provide adequate warmth on one's feet. A slipper is often needed.

So when choosing one's indoor footwear, keep in mind the following things.

INDOORSMAN SLIPPER GUIDE

1. *Type:* Open-Heel Slippers

    a. *Description:* These slippers are usually crafted with a fabric upper that covers the top of the foot and the toes but leaves the heel open.

    b. *When to wear:* These are not recommended for the everyday indoors, which is why, historically, they are often distributed in expensive hotels, spas, and hospitals. If keeping the feet warm is a priority, these do not suffice, as they are the equivalent of wrapping sewing thread around your foot while leaving your heel naked.

2. *Type:* Closed Slippers

    a. *Description:* These are designed with a fabric heel component, which prevents the foot from sliding out. So the foot easily slips in, but it does not so easily slip out. These are marvels of Indoorsmanship.

    b. *When to wear:* These are the most common form of everyday Indoorsman slipper—if, that is, one defines slippers in a more conventional sense. Depending on their material and thickness, they can do well in keeping one's feet warm.

3. *Type:* Slipper Boots

    a. *Description:* These are designed to be slippers but look like boots.

Generally only worn by female Indoorsmen, they are typically furry boots with a fleece or soft lining and a soft rubber sole.

b. *When to wear:* These kinds of slippers break the mold a bit for many reasons, not the least of which is they are perfectly acceptable for wearing outside, much like sheepskin boots. For that reason, though they technically fall into the slipper category, a strong recommendation for their indoor use simply cannot be offered here.

4. *Type:* The Sneaky Slipper

a. *Description:* Sometimes the Avid Indoorsman will use a sneaker as a slipper, but only if this shoe meets a specific set of criteria. Certain shoes (such as Sketchers) generally meet these standards, as they are not made for running, basketball, or any other physical activity.

b. *When to wear:* Wearing an extremely comfortable sneaker as a slipper is generally a practice saved for certain shoes in your life that you do not wear for physical activity. Usually, they are the ones you've only tied once, and then you simply slip them on and off like a slipper. Sneakers as slippers are great for lounging in an indoor space for long amounts of time because they allow one to briefly step outside to check the mail or let the dog out without having to change shoes.

5. *Type:* Socks and Sandals as Slippers

a. *Description:* Much like the sneaker slipper, socks and sandals can function as slippers of sorts. While some athletes adhere to this practice in the form of wearing socks with slides (flip-flop-style sandals with a top strap) over their socks as warm-up footwear, the Indoorsman may combine socks with sandals at any time and in any situation.

b. *When to wear:* The non-Indoorsman would advise you never to wear socks and sandals, so this is yet another moment when the Indoorsman paradigm goes against the grain of conventional thought. So, while socially unacceptable, if you simply try it, you will find there is no more comfortable footwear than socks and sandals. It marries the comfort of flip-flops and the warmth of socks into an utterly delightful footwear marriage. If you choose a toe-thong-style of flip-flop, you may experience discomfort (beyond the social kind) for a few minutes until the sock stretches and adjusts to the thong between your toes. If you can endure the awkwardness, though, you will choose socks and sandals every time.

6. *Type:* Novelty Slippers

a. *Description:* This type of slipper must be mentioned since the point of this exercise is to be exhaustive in exploring all slipper-related options, but for the most part, a novelty slipper will not make your everyday  footwear list. These slippers are usually made of soft and colorful materials, and they may come in the shapes of animals, one's favorite team mascot, cartoon characters, and the like.

b. *When to wear:* Novelty slippers are generally for Novice Indoorsmen, but they can actually be quite comfortable, much to everyone's surprise. This is probably due to all of the excess fluff that is sewn and stuffed around them in various shapes and sizes. This fluff actually works to better insulate the slipper, causing it to possess superior warming power. But even the confident Indoorsman will rarely don a novelty slipper, simply because of the very real negative social implications. If you must, do so when you are completely alone or around close friends or relatives from whom you are already accustomed to receiving ridicule and shame.

5. INDOORSMAN SITUATIONAL CLOTHING ETHICS

It behooves us to briefly delve into a few topics regarding the actual professional and personal life of the Indoorsman in terms of the choices he should make in clothing.

A. Office Appropriate

Consider the following questions and concepts:

- The truth is, most people, even if they work predominantly at their laptop in the safety of their indoor domain, will have to venture into the outside world for meetings, projects, or assignments related to inter-actions with other people. In most cases, these people will be your employer, either by means of their position in the company for which you both work or as your client or customer for a creative project or service you are providing. Therefore, it is imperative you make a good impression on whomever you are meeting.

- This does not mean you must disregard all the other Indoorsman wisdom related to one's choice of attire, but it does mean you may have to temporarily suspend some of your more natural or desirable fashion tendencies. Yes, this may feel like a betrayal of your truest self, but you are capable. The world is a difficult place, and sometimes you have to overcome.

- Depending upon the type of business, meeting, or office you are entering, there are items that are generally considered office appropriate. The first is slacks—these are non–blue jean, nonsweatpants pants (sometimes called dress pants or khakis). When possible, avoid khakis, but they will be necessary in extreme situations. Button-down shirts (which, oddly enough, you actually button up) generally go best with slacks. If your meeting is with a tech company or client, jeans (non-ripped) will often be considered appropriate, but be careful. Obviously, you would never want to wear flip-flops, socks and sandals, or slippers of any sort.

- *Stocking caps or toboggans.* Your geography probably determines your choice of word for this article of clothing. Southerners tend to call the hats that snugly wrap around your head and ears toboggans, while those outside the South consider a toboggan to be a sled used in the snow.[1] Regardless, this is another key piece of clothing utilized by both Indoorsmen and Outdoorsmen alike. And, once again, the general application is the same: warmth for one's head. But some Indoorsmen consider the stocking cap to be

---

1. If you are a non-Southerner, please do not wear a snow sled on your head. It will not keep your head warm, and you are just asking for a nasty and unnecessary head wound.

acceptable year-round headwear. This is especially true of musicians, who often wear stocking caps as a means to avoid washing their hair for weeks. The weather can be 100 degrees (Fahrenheit) outside, but their stocking caps stay in place. No one knows how these fringe Indoorsmen manage to avoid sweating profusely due to the constant warmth being added to their noggins via their toboggans—it is another Indoorsman mystery. In general, most true Indoorsmen save the stocking cap for cold temperatures. But they are willing to wear them indoors during these seasons, unlike their Outdoorsman counterparts.

6. THE INDOORSMAN'S HYGIENE

As the master of his domain, the Avid Indoorsman is a stickler about personal hygiene. But he may paint between the conventional lines of personal hygiene with a somewhat wider brush—not to be confused with a hairbrush. He rarely uses one, opting instead for that just-rolled-out-of-bed look.

A. Philosophy

In terms of this area of his life, the philosophical lines between health and appearance are significantly blurred in places. This is not to say that the Indoorsman suffers from vanity or overlooks the basic necessities of fitness in order to focus upon his appearance; it merely means he believes that a healthy appearance will result from a healthy lifestyle. Consequently, he also believes the inverse of this statement to be as true and reliable.

So, then, specifically concerning the matter of hygiene as it relates to both health and personal appearance, the Indoorsman's focus lies in two key areas: showering and beard care.

B. Showering

Perhaps no other area of the Indoorsman philosophy is better mirrored and thus reflected by an actual indoor space than the shower. If the indoors is a sanctuary, the shower is its inner sanctum. It is the room in which Avid Indoorsmen desire to spend the most amount of time, often to the chagrin of their spouses and utility companies.

The shower is a uniquely special room to the Indoorsman because it embodies everything he values most: seclusion, comfort, warmth, white noise, and darkness (if the shower and/or the shower technique implemented allow for such). It is the place where he rests, contemplates, dreams, and even bathes himself to either prepare for the coming day or decompress from the day's activities just completed. If the indoors is a place to get away from the outside world, the shower is the place to get away from the inside world as well.

Historical sources reveal that early restrooms were referred to as water closets. Even if these didn't include showers, modern bathrooms would do well to recapture such an appropriate name because it is reflective of all the best attributes of the shower sanctuary. From a seclusion standpoint, the Indoorsman knows that only his spouse is permitted to invade his shower space, which means that everyone else in the house must respect the privacy of this paradisiacal escape. While entertaining guests, in-laws, or other family members, most people reach a point when they

wish they could hide in a closet and have a moment to gather themselves. The water closet provides just such a socially acceptable place to do so.

In terms of comfort, there is nothing like an enclosed indoor space that is being cascaded with piping hot water. Yes, this can be expensive in terms of electricity and water utility bills, but the Avid Indoorsman sees this as a worthwhile investment in his emotional well-being and mental sanity. In other words, a few more dollars spent on a few extra hot showers is well worth every penny.

The coup d'état of the stressful day is the addition of a shower bench or seat, upon which the Indoorsman may sit, rest, think, and relax beneath the shower's hot stream. Such a seat need not be extravagant or even overly comfortable, because it is the literal act of sitting in the shower that is the ultimate luxury. What else could a man want in life but to be enclosed in a private space that is warm and steamy while also being able to take a seat?

Respected indoors historians have long held that the famous early twentieth-century sculpture known as *The Thinker* by Auguste Rodin was actually skillfully hewn for the purpose of clearly identifying an Indoorsman who was enjoying the sanctuary of his shower. After all, why else would a man be sitting so comfortably yet obviously so introspectively in the nude? It makes perfect sense that this time-honored image of philosophy and personal discovery is actually a rare glimpse into what all Avid Indoorsmen experience in their own showers: emotional respite and unparalleled mental acuity.

So, then, why was the shower component of this priceless piece not included in the sculpture? Because sculpting a stone shower (complete with flowing water) around *The Thinker* would have blocked the view of the statue itself. In other words, to give *The Thinker* the privacy any Indoorsman seeks in the shower, one would have to remove all visual access to the piece itself. Also, adding a water feature would have caused erosion of the stone over time, as well as exorbitant utility bills for the museums or local municipalities where this sculpture and all of its international replicas are displayed.

So, then, it is difficult to know the exact place where the Indoorsman's mental health, personal hygiene, and physical fitness converge, but the best guess is the shower. That is why one must understand at least the basics of proper Indoorsman shower etiquette.

INDOORSMAN SHOWER ETIQUETTE

1. *Lock the bathroom door.* Otherwise, unwanted family members (especially your children) will barge into the bathroom to ask such questions as, "Are you taking a shower?" or "How long are you going to be in there?" These impositions can be detrimental to your sustained mental state of restfulness and contemplation, causing you to have to start the shower over again. A locked door will often deter unwanted intruders.

2. *Turn off the lights and turn up the heat.* Perhaps it is an instinctive return to the dark, warm safety of the womb, but a restorative shower experience happens best in hot water and darkness. If there is a window in the bathroom, then true darkness will be hard to achieve, so you may want to wait until nighttime or install a retractable blackout shade. If the bathroom is pitch-black, your eyes should adjust in 35 to 65 seconds. So, in the meantime, be careful not to knock all of the shower accessories onto the floor. Using a smartphone light can help one get oriented without disturbing the delicate ambience.

3. *Sit down.* As we have learned, sitting down affords one the best use of quality shower time. Not everyone is fortunate enough to have a seat, but don't let that stop you. You can sit on the floor of the shower just as easily. Just pay attention to any tingling or numbness in your legs and feet, which means you have been sitting on the hard tile too long and you are cutting off your circulation.

4. *Bring a drink.* It may seem counterintuitive, but having access to a cold or hot drink can enhance one's shower experience (lukewarm drinks rarely produce the same effects). Obviously, open mugs or bottles are problematic due to their susceptibility to the shower water. If you must use them, while not drinking, place them on the tub/shower frame above the showerhead—in a safe location where they won't fall on your head. Otherwise, an insulated tumbler with a lid works perfectly to keep the drink temperature regulated and unwanted water out. You

can put this kind of container in the shower caddie between drinks—
not to be confused with a regular caddie, who may bring you a golf
club but not a drink in the shower.

5. *Beware of the loofah.* Many an Indoorsman uses a loofah rather than a
conventional washcloth, but only because their spouse insists. A loofah
cuts down on the need to make sure one has a washcloth, as it can be
used for months on end. But extensive use can cause the fabric of the
loofah to unravel a bit. This may cause the sharp epicenter of the loofah
to be exposed, and if the Indoorsman unknowingly uses it in a dark
shower, it can cause severe lacerations in some sensitive areas. Perhaps
that is why the term *loofah*, translated from its original Latin origins,
actually means "lovely razor sponge."

6. *Pay attention to the curtain behind the man.* All showers are not created
equal, although if the bathroom is free of other people and the water
is hot, they can all equally
provide an indoor sanctuary.
Some showers have glass doors
while others have curtains.
A curtained shower is fully
respectable, but a rookie
Indoorsman mistake is to leave
the bottom of the curtain
outside of the tub or shower
floor. This can ruin your
moment of solace, because
the longer you spend in the
water closet, the longer water
will have been running down
the curtain and pooling, even
flooding the bathroom floor.

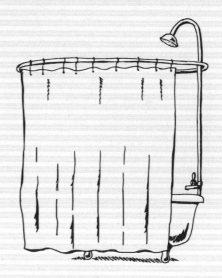

Evaluation of the Need to Bathe

In terms of actual hygiene, a shower is the most common form of Indoorsman bathing. Obviously, however, a shower means so much more than simply an opportunity for cleanliness. To that end, true Indoorsmen can skip showers for lengths of time that might be considered socially unacceptable in non-Indoorsman circles, that is, normal civilization.

So if an Indoorsman does not need a moment of sanctuary to gather his thoughts or escape the outside world—or perhaps the other rooms of his house—he may or may not choose to take a shower for hygienic purposes. Multiple variables factor into this decision-making process, and this sort of decision should not be made in isolation, even though isolation is an Indoorsman's default state. Simply put, when in doubt about whether it's time to take a shower, use the following chart.

Indoorsman Situation	Level of Shower Need (5 being the highest)
Woke up on a normal day but nothing planned	1 (no shower needed at this time)
No physical activity today but no shower yesterday	2 (shower might help but optional)
Played video games all day (no shower for two days)	3 (shower or keep avoiding people)
Had sizzling fajitas delivered to house and ate them	4 (shower soon or smell like fajitas)
Assembled furniture from IKEA, sweated down	5 (shower must occur right now)

C. Beard Care

The other major area of hygiene for the Indoorsman is beard care. Obviously, this area tends to be more relevant to male Indoorsmen than female. This is one component of Indoorsmanship in which stereotypes are ripe for defying. Over the centuries there has always been a sense that only Outdoorsmen are known for epic beards. In fact, even in the modern age, white-collar jobs have tended to prohibit employees from quality beard management, requiring a clean shave. Thus, up to now, it has been rare to happen upon a high school teacher or coach, an IRS agent, or a postal worker sporting a majestic beard.

One might think that the standard policeman's mustache is the exception to these rules, but a mustache does not a beard make any more than wearing Michael Jordan cologne makes one able to reverse dunk a basketball. In fact, no respectable Indoorsman will wear a mustache unless, as in the case of a police officer, it is the only form of facial hair allowed by his employee handbook.

So, then, what constitutes a good beard? How does an Indoorsman's beard differ from an Outdoorsman's beard?

To begin, a good beard is one that meets the following three criteria: 1) intentionally maintained, 2) trimmed (even if at a very long length), and 3) devoid of food particles. In fact, following these directives will not only help the Indoorsman possess a quality beard but will also keep him from inadvertently growing an Outdoorsman's beard.

First, let's deal with the intentional maintenance of one's beard. The key word here is "intentional." The Outdoorsman often lives as if he is unaware he has a beard at all, as if there is no bulky, smelly, discombobulated mass of whiskers and food flowing down from beneath his chin. The Indoorsman, on the other hand, lives with an acute awareness of his beard, and such a mental disposition is indeed half the battle.

Second, the Indoorsman allows his beard awareness to lead him to regular trimmings. Again, the trimming of one's beard is not indicative of its length. It simply means that the intentional thought toward the beard leads one to be mindful of, to the point of tending to, its uniformity. Uniformity and consistency are the goals of good beard maintenance, and keeping the beard neatly trimmed is essential to both.

Finally, a good beard must be free from all foreign particles, namely, food. Yes, the Indoorsman is steeped in his own form of indoor ruggedness, but that does not mean that he should settle for shrapnel in his beard. From excess Cheez-Its crumbs to long, stringy remnants of melted cheese that never made it from the chili bowl to the piehole, the beard should never be treated like an extra food strainer. Even if one opts for fewer showers, one must always be mindful of keeping the beard free from debris.

Plenty of Indoorsmen do not wear a beard at all, which is a fine choice to make in the way of indoor living. But if this is the choice you make, just know that shaving will be a perpetual practice in your life. The good news is that it is completely acceptable to constantly be cycling through various levels of beardedness and clean-shavenness. In other words, the amount of time you spend between trips outside of your house may determine your frequency of shaving.

The following facial hair reference guide will help you know what to do when you encounter various shave-related scenarios.

FACIAL HAIR REFERENCE GUIDE

Your Status	Status of Facial Hair	Action You Should Take
Hanging out alone	Peach fuzz	Always shave peach fuzz
Hanging out alone	Light stubble to full beard	No shaving necessary
Hanging with wife	Light stubble	No shaving necessary
Hanging with wife	Heavy stubble	Listen for complaints during kissing
Hanging with wife	Full beard	If beard is agreed upon, skip shaving. If beard is disputed, consider shaving.
Hanging with family	Light stubble	No shaving necessary
Hanging with family	Heavy stubble	Shave at your own discretion, but expect criticism from your mother
Hanging with family	Full beard	If beard is not a common thing, prepare for group discussion about it
Hanging with buddies	Light stubble	Consider shaving simply to avoid ridicule for being a wuss
Hanging with buddies	Heavy stubble	No shaving necessary
Hanging with buddies	Full beard	Expect admiration from friends
Hanging with anyone	Mustache	There is never an instance in which a solo mustache is appropriate

Finally, the Indoorsman wants to avoid an Outdoorsman-style beard at all costs. To the Novice Indoorsman, especially when he is young and excited about the prospect of growing facial hair at all, the differences between the two can be overlooked or disregarded, resulting in social ridicule or worse. The following chart will help you know the various types of Indoorsman and Outdoorsman beards.

INDOORSMAN ALTERNATIVES TO OUTDOORSMAN BEARDS

Outdoorsman Beard 1: The Eager Fuzzbucket

This beard is often grown on long camping or hiking trips by Novice Outdoorsman. Any Indoorsman knows that if one's facial hair has any sort of fuzz consistency to it and one is going into public, it must be shaved until actual whiskers appear.

Indoorsman Beard Alternative 1: The Patient Apprentice

The Indoorsman philosophy of bearddom takes into account the awkward fuzz stage of beard growing by regulating this stage to the obvious location: the secluded indoors. In other words, the Indoorsman way is to avoid contact with the public until one's beard becomes whisker worthy. This process involves movie marathons, video game playing, ordering only carry-out, and seeing only close friends and family members during this time of peach fuzz quarantine.

Outdoorsman Beard 2: The Side Canyon

This beard is often grown by older Outdoorsmen and features a strange shaving pattern that rounds down the cheek area and off to a thinner line, avoiding the obvious natural growing pattern.

Indoorsman Beard Alternative 2: The Normal Guy

The alternative to this beard is so painfully obvious: Just let the beard grow in naturally and do not shave it down on the cheeks. The best beard is the most simple and natural one, so never be afraid to let nature take its course with your face—with consistent maintenance and trimmings, of course.

Outdoorsman Beard 3: The Face Mullet

This beard is often grown by Avid Outdoorsmen who do not mind carrying a constant tripping hazard and grease trap that's connected to their bodies. This beard can actually cloak undetected food particles, dust mites, and the occasional rodent for days on end.

Indoorsman Beard Alternative 3:
The Hipster

If ever there ws any confusion between two types of beards, it is here. The Hipster is different for a variety of reasons. Obviously, it is intentionally trimmed and not left to grow wildly like volunteer kudzu down one's face. Also, Indoorsmen understand the responsibility of such beard girth, so they constantly brush, clean, and generally maintain their bearded greatness with a sense of masculine urgency. No food particles are left to chance. The final and most distinguishable difference is the use of a high-priced beard oil to achieve a hipster sheen. Face Mullets are also oily, but for much less desirable and alarming reasons that are better left to the imagination.

Outdoorsman Beard 4:
The John the Baptist

This beard name means no disrespect to its namesake, but in terms of fashion and functionality, John the Baptist did live alone in the desert while wearing clothes made of camel hair and eating locusts dipped in honey—which probably translated into huge clumps of sticky dead bug parts scattered throughout his huge beard. So unless you're going to find yourself baptizing people in muddy river water all day, this one's definitely not for you.

Indoorsman Beard Alternative 4:
The Telecaster Master

There are many varied fields of Indoorsmanship, not the least of which is that of the musician. The Telecaster Master is the perfect alternative to the uncivilized John the Baptist beard. It pays homage to the same sense of one's internal wilderness without leaving one's facial hair to its own cruel, twisted fate like some untamed whiskered shrew lurking on one's face. The Telecaster Master says, "Look at this beard! Like me, it's unpredictable and undomesticated but not feral."

Outdoorsman Beard 5:
The Handlebarbarian

This beard has been referenced by many others because of its unmistakable shape, which vividly mirrors motorcycle handlebars. This look could not be further from an Indoorsman mind-set. There is no place for leather chaps, skulls and/or crossbones designs, or painted fiery flames upon the body and/or vehicle of an Indoorsman.

Indoorsman Beard Alternative 5:
The Subtle Goatee

This beard should not be attempted insouciantly. The goatee is not always an acceptable form of beardedness, but it is mentioned here as an alternative to the atrocious Handlebarbarian. Though this style was pretty much retired from social acceptance after the late 1990s, the modern Indoorsman may still temporarily sport a Subtle Goatee at times, especially if he needs more time to grow his beard than a beard quarantine will afford him. But this goatee must be trimmed short at all times and never be allowed to grow more than 0.25 to 0.35 inches in length. Also, it must be a complete goatee and never devoid of a mustache. In fact, this is the only instance in which a mustache is acceptable outside of a full beard. But exercise wisdom and caution with the goatee. It is not for everyone and can quickly get out of hand.

AN INDOORSMAN'S GUIDE TO MISCELLANEOUS SITUATIONS

The Constitution is the [indoor] guide which I will never abandon.

GEORGE WASHINGTON

Situational awareness is a key to survival and success in this world. The same rings true for one's awareness of the appropriate application of Indoorsman principles to varying circumstances. The following theories and explanations will hopefully prepare you for a multiplicity of scenarios.

1. ERGONOMIC CONVENIENCE

Every Indoorsman must learn to make decisions regarding how to arrange an ergonomically enhanced indoor space.

A. Couch

The couch is an indispensable feature of any indoor domain. It can function for the Indoorsman in his ideal state of social isolation, providing a place for him (along with his spouse and children, when applicable) to lie down, watch TV, take a much-deserved

nap, catch up on his phone, play video games, or even work on his laptop before dozing off.

Functionality

The couch can also function as the perfect space for those moments when the Indoorsman must host guests. While organizations such as fraternities comprised of generally extroverted members may elect a social chair (a chairperson in charge of planning and implementing various social activities), the Indoorsman considers his couch to be the social chair—a literal place where more than one person can sit comfortably.

General Positioning

The couch is often the centerpiece of the indoor space, but it cannot simply be placed at the center of the indoor space. It must be properly positioned if its full potential is to be met.

The single most important key to couch positioning is its adjacency and angle in relation to the TV. For starters, never place your couch on a wall too close to the perpendicular wall where the TV hangs. Otherwise, you will constantly have to look up and toward the direction of the TV. Slide the couch down the wall, away from the direction of the TV, to help with this problem. When possible, the best couch positioning is directly opposite the TV, even if the couch must be placed in the middle of the room or against a wall.

Angle

In general, most normal home entertainment scenarios function best when the Indoorsman is watching the TV at a 30-degree angle. Note that many professional theaters design their space for a 40-degree viewing angle.

Distance

The other key to couch-TV placement is distance. The following chart will help you determine the optimal distance based upon the size of your television (assuming you are viewing it at a 30-degree angle).[1]

Screen Size	Recommended Couch-TV Distance	Indoorsman Rating (5 being highest)
25 inches	3.4 linear feet	*Not deserving of rating*
30 inches	4.1 linear feet	1 (30 inches? That's a laptop, not a TV)
35 inches	4.8 linear feet	1.5
40 inches	5.5 linear feet	2
45 inches	6.1 linear feet	2.5
50 inches	6.8 linear feet	3
55 inches	7.5 linear feet	3.5
60 inches	8.2 linear feet	4
65 inches	8.9 linear feet	4.5
70 inches	9.5 linear feet	5 (Ideal!)
75 inches	10.2 linear feet	4.8 (Beware of pretentiousness)

1. Figures for various distances and angles adapted from https://www.rtings.com/tv/reviews/by-size/size-to-distance -relationship.

Main Auxiliary Issue: Drink Placement

While *eating* on a couch is a challenge that most people learn to conquer at a young age, only Avid Indoorsmen ever truly learn how to successfully manage *drinking* on the couch. While some couches are crafted with built-in cup holders, it is more likely that your couch will not have this feature. Furthermore, an unexpected spill can quickly ruin a beautiful indoor moment, so here are some ideas that will help with drink placement.

1. Keep your drink on a coffee table or side table. This is the best option if your coffee table or side table is close enough to the couch to easily reach without having to sit up too far.

2. Place your drink on the floor directly against the bottom of the couch. This method works for the isolated Indoorsman but can be perilous for those who have children, who will be instinctively drawn to your couch for the purpose of kicking over your drink.

3. Put your drink into a mug with a lid. Containers that keep liquids perpetually hot or cold (like a Yeti) can be ideal for this option. While there are mouth holes in the lids, in general, even if such containers tip over, they will not produce a large spill.[2]

Another Miscellaneous Concern: Leg Propping

Obviously, the ideal couch scenario is that you will be able to lie down, thus providing a natural position for your legs. But when you are sharing the couch with others, you may be forced to prop your legs on something else. The coffee table is the most obvious choice, but you must evaluate the consequences of such a decision. Will your coffee table easily break under the weight of your legs? Will there

---

2. Beware, because even though these Yeti-type containers are marvels of modern Indoorsmanship, you must resist the tendency to subconsciously default to normal drink thinking. In other words, just because your hot drink has sat there for an hour, you must remember that, due to the container's miraculous properties of insulation, it has not cooled down a single degree, as any other drink would. It is a matter of habit, but forgetting that your liquid is still as hot as the molten surface of the sun can cause you to unassumingly gulp when you should still be gingerly sipping. The results can be painfully disastrous and can ruin your casual couch respite.

be negative marital fallout to such a choice? Is the table close enough to the couch (or too close) to produce a comfortable leg-propping scenario?

If you choose to prop up your feet on a coffee table, at least have the decency to remove your shoes or wear slippers (see "Honorable Mentionables: Slippers" in chapter 7). This will be especially effective if your spouse is not home to witness your leg propping, because there should be no evidence in the form of mud, dirt, leaves, etc. left behind to betray your behavior. You might consider using an ottoman, which is a small padded footstool made for just such scenarios.[3]

B. Recliner

The couch may be the centerpiece of the indoor domain because it provides a comfortable gathering place for all who enter—like the fuselage of an airplane provides the area for seating for all the passengers—but the recliner is the Indoorsman's cockpit, an actual captain's chair.

Functionality

The recliner is a single seat generally reserved for the master of the Indoorsman domain, although anyone may sit in it at any given time. If the living room were a table, the recliner would be the head chair, the place where the main communication and flow of the room originates. Many Indoorsmen develop a deep, meaningful emotional attachment to this piece of furniture, which is something that generally does not happen with other furniture.

General Positioning

All the spacing and angular guidelines and suggestions that applied to the couch and its positioning in relation to the TV apply to the recliner as well. But unlike the couch, there are ergonomic issues related to the recliner, as it is not a stationary piece of furniture. By virtue of its name, a recliner is defined by its ability to recline; that is, to lean back and lift up the legs, which creates a reclined position for the person using the chair. The variable options related to one's reclining position must be evaluated carefully.

---

3. This kind of ottoman should not be confused with the ancient empire also known as Ottoman.

The Unreclined Position

This position is ideal for hosting guests, especially those whom you do not know that well. It can be socially awkward to initiate the sequence of transitioning the chair from an unreclined to a partially or fully reclined position in the presence of strangers, making you appear unrefined or aloof.[4] Otherwise, just use the recliner as a regular chair until the correct conditions for reclining are met.

The Partially Reclined Position

The partially reclined position is defined by raising the footrest portion of the recliner but not leaning back. This position mimics the use of an ottoman and is also ideal for hosting guests, which means that it is doubtful the TV will be turned on. You should not immediately raise the footrest but rather wait until the conversation has persisted for at least one hour. One does not want to look too comfortable when hosting other guests who do not have their own places to recline. If ottomans are available for the others in the room, you may bypass this one-hour rule.

The Fully Reclined Position

This position is defined by the full use of every feature the recliner affords its occupant, which means the footrest is raised and the chair is leaning back as far as it can go. This position is mostly reserved for watching TV, but it can also be used in the presence of those who reside in the house with you. In terms of hosting guests, if they are close friends or family and the environment is very casual, which generally means laughing is

---

4. One need only to recall the scene from *Sweet Home Alabama* where the character portrayed by Reese Witherspoon's Confederate reenactor father plops the mayor of New York down in his easy chair and sends her flailing backward into the fully reclined position. Awkward.

excessive, you may feel comfortable enough socially to also exercise full comfort physically in their presence.

2. TRANSPORTATION

It is obvious that the preference for living is to remain indoors, but life will most likely require you to temporarily vacate indoor spaces or at least travel between them. Fret not, because the advent of modern transportation has continued the historical Indoorsman legacy of always instinctively developing more convenient and efficient methodologies for moving from the outdoors to the indoors.

Yes, the various modes of transportation to which we have access today have obviously emerged out of a desire to move over large distances in a faster, more efficient manner. But the lesser-known purpose of modern transportation is to also minimize the amount of time away from one's primary indoor space—and by proxy, the outdoors—by creating mobile indoor spaces. These spaces can become familiar, comforting secondary indoor safe places for the Avid Indoorsman—a home away from home, but on wheels, tracks, or pockets of air (depending upon the method of transportation).

This is the reason that modern forms of transportation have become more and more ergonomically sound, comfortable, efficient, and technologically advanced. These are meant not just for *recreation* but also the *re-creation* of one's indoor space while you're away from the indoors.

A. Automobiles

Cars are obviously the most utilized mobile indoor space on the planet today. Unlike other forms of transportation, an automobile allows the Indoorsman to take his secondary indoor space anywhere he pleases with the simple turn of a steering wheel.

B. Indoorsman Automobile Recommendations

There really isn't any one ideal car for all Indoorsmen, but there certainly are features and trends that tend to characterize those vehicles that seem to work best in the Indoorsman paradigm.

The Unassuming Two-Door

These small cars are perfect for the compact Indoorsman heading to a college class, an Apple Store appointment, or a local oxygen bar. Small vehicles such as these are generally economical, especially if they are hybrids or electric, and they can even fit into the most impossibly snug parking spaces—such as those where Outdoorsmen have senselessly encroached over the clearly painted line with their enormous, boisterous, dual-exhaust diesel trucks. The joke's on them. Your two-door doesn't require a mortgage to own or a ladder to enter.

The Spunky Hatchback

A hatchback is the perfect vehicle for the Indoorsman who wants to remain in a small car and yet still be able to easily transport his gear. Such items could include photography equipment, musical instruments, and the like. Many people don't realize that a celebrated piece of literature arose from this vehicle type. Specifically, it was the tale of an obscure Indoorsman hermit who parked his station wagon in the basement of an ancient French cathedral. The story was originally titled *The Hatchback of Notre Dame* but was later adapted into its modern concept, *The Hunchback of Notre Dame*, by the suits in Hollywood.

The Minivan vs. the SUV

The cultural wars continue to rage on between the minivan and the SUV. Both vehicles are generally used by families with children, and while these families have much in common, there remains a sharp divide between them over this issue. An individual is either a minivan person or an SUV person—he or she cannot be both. Ironically, despite the malice between the two groups, both vehicles provide ideal Indoorsman transportation, as they are roomy enough in the interior to almost constitute an actual room. Captain's chairs,

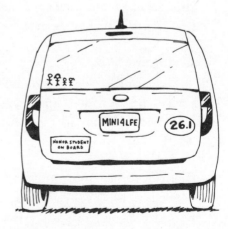

benches, Blu-ray players displaying movies from drop-down screens, and cup hold-ers are all reminiscent of the beloved amenities of one's living room, which is why they can be the ideal Indoorsman vehicle if used properly and with minimal bum-per stickers and decals (less than three total).[5]

The Sensible Truck

A common misconception about Indoorsmen is that they are unequivocally opposed to trucks on principle, but this is not at all accurate. Many Indoorsmen own and operate trucks, but they do so for the purpose of using the truck for its intended and practical uses. These uses include transporting items in the bed of the truck that will not fit into cars, minivans, or SUVs, as well as items that are too messy, dirty, or negatively odoriferous for an enclosed vehicular space. They may even own a 4x4 truck, but only if they live in an area where there are climate-related or geographical possibilities a 4x4 might be needed. These include areas where snowfall is common in the winter, mountainous areas, or areas where flood-ing is common.

---

5. The little family icon stickers (with one sticker per each family member) should count as one sticker in this evaluation, minus any accompanying pet stickers, which still count as additional stickers.

The most important philosophical truck distinction between an Indoorsman and an Outdoorsman is the idea that a truck is a statement of something unto itself. In other words, Outdoorsmen have been known to buy bigger, more expensive, louder trucks simply to make a public statement about their Outdoorsmanship. It is an overcompensation, to say the least. Their trucks can actually be a wonderful indoor space, but when they feel the need to have them tricked out, jacked up, slammed, or equipped with extremely loud mufflers that seem to muffle nothing so that everyone within a three-mile radius can hear them coming down the road, then the sensible purpose of the truck has been compromised, lost in a sea of self-proclaimed Outdoorsman stereotypes and rhetoric.

C. Other Forms of Ground Transportation

There will be certain times in the Indoorsman experience when situations arise that require transportation other than that provided by a motor vehicle. The following are a few examples.

Trains

Transportation by train has become a lesser-used option in the modern age, but the train still offers a unique indoor space for those who come all aboard. Passenger trains allow their Indoorsman passengers to view the beauty of the outdoors from the comfort of a climate-controlled railcar. While one cannot alter their course to another destination once a train has left the station, with proper planning and research (especially about dining and drink options), a train can still be a memorable indoors experience.

Public Transit

This method of transportation generally involves city buses but, in major cities, also includes subway trains. Neither of these is ideal for the Indoorsman, as he prefers to avoid crowds, but it does beat hoofing it through the outdoors, especially in extreme weather situations.

Other Possibilities to Avoid

In general, the Indoorsman way leans toward safest and most secure mode of transportation available that also offers supreme comfort and the best amenities possible. For the most part, this rules out scooters and mopeds, even though there are stereotypes about Indoorsmen, mainly those of the hipster variety riding them. Such persons, even if they are considered Indoorsmen, are generally not avid, to say the least. Other modes of day-to-day transportation that most Avid Indoorsmen will generally avoid are dogsleds, bicycles, skateboards, longboards, sailboards, horses, horse-drawn carriages, and two-person handcar-style railcars.

3. PET OWNERSHIP

As the Indoorsman's world has broadened in the late twentieth and early twenty-first centuries, it is now more common for one's indoor space to also include a non-human coinhabitant. Domesticated animals are all the rage, but how do they fit into a true Indoorsman paradigm? Can just any kind of animal function well in this lifestyle? What pitfalls (or pit bulls) should be avoided?

At first glance, the Indoorsman mind-set would seem to lean toward not owning a pet. After all, inviting a wild animal into one's treasured domain could be detrimental to that very space. Dander, feces, urine, and the destruction of furniture are the major concerns to be considered. But aren't these the same concerns one has when certain children (possibly our own) or family members enter our indoor space? How do we deal with them? We plan ahead. We communicate. We put down our newspapers long enough to actually put down newspaper on the floor.

While the best recommendation for avoiding indoor complications in these areas is to keep animals (and also certain people) out of your indoors, it is possible for the Avid Indoorsman to successfully own an indoor pet. In fact, the right pet can actually help clean up food messes on the floor like a living vacuum cleaner.

Furthermore, a pet can offer companionship and keep you from having to frequently engage with people. In this manner, the general introverted nature of the Indoorsman can be well served by the right kind of pet. You may even develop a voice for the animal and thus engage in conversation with it. It may sound weird at first, but many Indoorsmen engage in this practice in isolation, much as Tom Hanks did with Wilson the volleyball when they were stranded on a deserted island in the movie *Cast Away*.

So, then, pets most definitely have the potential to be compatible with the Avid Indoorsman's life. The key to choosing the right pet comes from educating oneself so that the best choices can be made before and also during the process.

A. Three Determining Factors for Choosing and Managing Indoor Pets

1. *The pet's outdoor needs and desires.* As an Indoorsman, it would make little to no sense to acquire a pet that prefers to be outdoors. If your pet is constantly bolting

for the door every time you open it, as if freedom and happiness awaited them outside, then perhaps your pet is not of the Indoorsman persuasion. This includes dogs who require long walks outdoors instead of simply doing their business and returning to their indoor paradise.

2. *The pet's natural compatibility with your indoor space.* This is where many would-be Indoorsmen go awry. If you bring an animal into your indoor space whose very presence destroys that space, then further evaluation of your own logic needs to be conducted. Piles of fur, the chewing of furniture legs, the chewing of human legs, and the like indicate that your pet is probably more suited for the outdoors or for the home of an Outdoorsman.

3. *The pet's compatibility with the Indoorsman.* Most people are at least moderately familiar with the fact that people can form bonds of companionship with animals. Many an Outdoorsman has gotten dust in his eye[6] when his hunting dog, Old Blue, finally succumbed to old age or eventually just kept right on hunting into the old wild blue yonder instead of returning home. For the Indoorsman, this bond is also very important, as the space he is sharing with this animal is somewhat sacred to him. The best recommendation for this kind of pet is one that is:

Nonyippy or barky. If you or your guests can't walk through the house without being screamed at in canine, what's the point really?

Chill. While small dogs can be cute, small and hyper dogs can drive you to the point of insanity. If they can never stop jumping excessively, then are they really mirroring your own minimalistic-exercise philosophy?

Nonshedding. If you can't wear a black shirt on your own couch because you are constantly covered in discarded fur, perhaps you should rethink your indoor pet decision. This is not meant to be insensitive to the value of your pet, who may be the best animal who has ever lived. In cases where keeping the pet is the obvious choice, resign yourself to a life of vacuuming rather than a life of being covered in discarded animal dander.

Hypoallergenic. If a certain animal can, at any moment, cause you or your guests to suddenly break out into hives or fits of violent sneezing, then perhaps it doesn't belong indoors. Just saying. Yes, this sounds extreme and revolutionary to many

---

6. Getting dust in one's eye is a classic Outdoorsman method for explaining away the presence of tears.

misguided pet owners in the world today, but housing animals that cause major allergy flare-ups among humans is just another result of poor Indoorsmanship education and training in the modern world.

B. Five Most Recommended Pets for the Indoorsman

1. *Dogs.* Above all else, Indoorsmen choose dogs as their indoor pets. It is recommended that you choose a small- or medium-sized dog unless your indoor domain is extra spacious. Certain breeds do not shed, are generally calm, and are hypoallergenic, including bichons, poodles, and the like. Again, do your own research.

2. *Monkeys.* These are less common in the United States, but the right kind of monkey can actually enhance your indoor experience. The wrong kind of monkey can start a global epidemic—so choose wisely.

3. *Goldfish.* Goldfish can be difficult to play with but not impossible. The good news is that a goldfish will not invade or affect your indoor space in any way unless something goes terribly wrong.

4. *Guinea pigs.* In general, the Indoorsman prefers to keep rodents out of his indoor space, but there are exceptions. Of all possible domesticated rodents one could own, the most recommended would be guinea pigs. They can be contained in their own indoor space, so like the goldfish, encroachment into the greater indoor space is easily controlled or minimalized. Guinea pigs actually perform little hops in the air, also known as popcorning, but avoid feeding them popcorn, as they could choke and die.

5. *Cats.* Obviously, this is a joke. No serious Indoorsman would ever allow a cat into his indoor domain. Any animal that sprays its urine, causes allergic reactions for 10 to 15 percent of the population, defecates in a box multiple times before the box requires removal, is commonly known to play with its owners by scratching their face and eyes, and in general doesn't really like humans has no place in the indoors.

4. SPORTS

After a particularly blazing June doubleheader, Babe Ruth remarked, "I wish baseball was played indoors."[7] Even back then, he recognized the tension that exists between Indoorsmanship and sportsmanship. The following are a few guidelines for navigating this tension.

A. Sports-Resistant Indoorsmen

Some Indoorsmen view sports as extensions of the Outdoorsman's worldview and are thus not just disinterested but downright apoplectic toward the whole concept. They see modern athletics and the billion-dollar industries surrounding them as a culturally contrived means to exclude those who do not have a natural propensity for athletics. This particular brand of Indoorsman is commonly referred to as a sports-resistant Indoorsman.

Obviously, the vast majority of sports fans are not all physically equipped to actually participate in the college or professional sport they follow. This is why an unkempt man in a dirty tank top and tighty-whities weighing in excess of 300 pounds can drop his plate of hot wings to vehemently scream at the television simply because another man—whom he has never met and who happens to be running at full speed while carrying a piece of pigskin and has a history of working out with weights, daily performing complex calisthenics, and practicing football plays eight hours a day while also attending college classes—is mere inches away from being able to avoid being violently attacked by another semiprofessional beast of an athlete. To the sports-resistant Indoorsman, there is a cognitive dissonance to such a cultural trend that simply cannot be ignored or dismissed.

The sports-resistant Indoorsman not only does not feel insecure when someone asks him the score of a certain game or about the replay of a certain spectacular athletic play, he will often make fun of the sport itself as a rebuttal. You can recognize his version of Indoorsmanship because he will wield derogatory statements like, "Super Bowl? Is that a football game?" or "Sports ball? Sure, who doesn't love sports ball!"

---

7. There is a solid chance he did not actually say this, but he probably would have if he could have read this book.

B. Sports-Interested Indoorsmen

Not all Indoorsmen are sports resistant, however. In fact, most Indoorsmen possess at least a nominal interest in athletics, even if this involves only keeping up with the most popular topics, games, and scores. In most cases, they are at least familiar with the rules, strategies, and general objectives of the games themselves. Generally, they do not possess the skills to engage in these sports at a competitive level, but they do enjoy them with their friends and family.

In terms of playing sports, they will participate on a recreational level, obviously preferring indoor sports, such as basketball, racquetball, bowling, indoor soccer, dodgeball, wiffle ball, and curling.

But in terms of their interest in the culture of sports, their indoor technological advancements offer them everything they need at their fingertips. By using various apps on their smartphones, they can keep up with scores, recruiting, press releases, coaching and personnel changes, trades, firings, and the like. They can also take control of their own teams through the advent of fantasy sports, a true Indoorsman advancement.

Above all else, sports-interested Indoorsmen enjoy watching sporting events live from the comfort of their own indoor domain. In fact, the more years a person grows in Indoorsmanship, the greater likelihood he or she will prefer watching a game on their own television than actually venturing into the outdoor hassles of crowds, parking, ticket scalping, and other less-than-desirable activities. Some have even been known to turn down free tickets in favor of staying home and watching the game on a high-definition television, which is also generally close to the kitchen where various game day sundries abound.

5. TATTOOS

Getting inked is a common practice in the modern world. While the process is not for everyone, as it does involve needles and is very expensive, many would-be Indoorsmen decide to pursue a tattoo.

The first thing to remember is that a tattoo is *permanent*. Adding something to your body when you are 18 years old that will still be with you when you are 81 years old should be a sobering prospect—and quite literally should only be done when one is completely sober. Many a person has regretted tattoo choices made in moments when they were under the influence of either an ingested substance or a particularly unwise group of friends.

Since a tattoo is indeed permanent, Indoorsman wisdom contends that one might consider waiting until they are 30 years old to get one. Yes, this seems extreme to people in their twenties, but if they do live into their eighties, then simple mathematics would support the idea of not putting something on your body in the first twenty-fifth percentile of your life that will last for the next seventy-fifth percentile. If one still desires the same tattoo at age 30, then it is safe to assume it is something one is serious about.

Another key piece of wisdom here, especially for the younger Indoorsman, is to select an inconspicuous location for the tattoo. Avoid the neck, face, hands, lips (yes, that is a thing), and lower arms, as these are highly visible and could even prevent you from landing a job ten years from now—and your ten-year-older self may be pretty upset with you if you do not consider his future existence and opinions. Wise locations include the shoulder, the calf, the upper arm, and possibly the underside of the wrist.

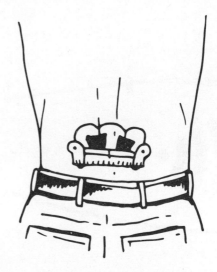

In terms of design choice, here are

a few things all Indoorsmen (and honestly, all humans) should probably avoid, as well as some ideas that work well with the Indoorsman mind-set.

INDOORSMAN TATTOO GUIDE

Avoid These No Matter What	Consider These with Caution
Barbed wire (of any sort)	Wi-Fi bars icon
Anything that covers a major muscle group	Favorite quote from *Seinfeld* or *The Office*
Your favorite team's mascot flexing	A tasteful Star Trek badge on your chest
Name of current boyfriend/girlfriend	Favorite Scripture reference
Your favorite *Real Housewives* catchphrase	A subtle couch across your lower back
Nickleback lyrics of any kind	Your Wi-Fi password hidden in plain sight

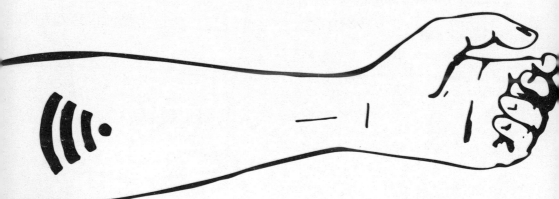

6. HOBBIES

As we have learned, Indoorsmanship is a vast discipline with many variables and degrees of implementation, mastery, and interest. The Indoorsman can be involved in any number of hobbies, including but not limited to the following.

A. Hobby Number 1: Wikipedia Editor

Many an Indoorsman has long dreamed of the opportunity to use his or her wealth of knowledge to correct others in an impersonal environment. If this is you, lending the World Wide Web your expertise as a Wikipedia editor is most definitely a hobby (at least) that you should pursue. Any contributor to this online encyclopedia is technically referred to as a Wikipedian, or more formally, an editor. Most Wikipedians are volunteers, which indicates the kind of screening process that at least promises some level of success.

B. Hobby Number 2: Yoga

If you ever drive past a yoga studio or watch one of the many commercials that utilize that setting on television, you have noticed that those who participate in yoga appear to be relaxed and even centered in themselves (not necessarily to be confused with self-centered, although both can be accomplished simultaneously, but you probably would be too focused on yourself to notice).

At any rate, yoga is a worthy endeavor for the Indoorsman, but beware the impressions you may have of it—and not just regarding yoga pants. While the yoga students you see on TV appear so relaxed, just know that holding plank, downward dog, or any other yoga move besides the warm-up breathing will soon deliver a level of crippling pain, cramping, and sweating throughout your body in a manner you once thought only reserved for wartime torture. But you should try it, and as your yoga instructor will repeatedly remind you with a smile, "Just relax."

C. Hobby Number 3: 3D Printing

If someone from the past could travel to our time and witness a 3D printer at work, they would probably decry it as witchcraft. It is indeed a type of craft, just not of the witching kind. If you can afford a 3D printer, then this manufacturing process that creates a solid, three-dimensional physical object from a digital design by adding layers of material onto layers of material is as perfect a hobby as any human can find. You may even decide to 3D print a few extra friends who won't interrupt you while you're watching Netflix. Be creative.

D. Hobby Number 4: Crossword Puzzles

A good crossword puzzle most definitely affords the Indoorsman a moment to himself so as to pan the frigid waters of his popular lexicon for vernacular nuggets of gold. While there are digital options for this hobby, most crossworders (not to be confused with CrossFitters) still prefer the antiquated but rewarding process of taking pen to paper.

E. Hobby Number 5: Fantasy Sports

The name is a little deceptive, as one might envision fantasy sports to involve a team of jersey-wearing dwarfs squaring off against their archrivals, the Elite Elves, as they gallop toward each other on the backs of angry minotaurs in order to advance a flaming magical orb past a certain painted line on a uniquely striped field somewhere in Middle Earth or Mordor. Fantasy sports is actually when you enter a league with other friends, use a computer to draft real players from various sports teams, and utilize a unique scoring system that processes individual stats independent of a team's weekly wins or losses to determine a points-based winner. Though this is not thought of as cool as Mordor Mania, many Indoorsmen greatly enjoy fantasy sports.

F. Hobby Number 6: Learning a Foreign Language

Most people in the world speak more than one language, but it is sad that this is not the reality for most Americans. The Indoorsman, however, can skew the national statistics toward a favorable outcome by pursing bilingualism in the privacy of his or her own home. Numerous online courses, apps, and programs are available to help you in such an endeavor in your spare time. Just be cautious not to become one of those people who not-so-nonchalantly inserts their most recently acquired foreign terms in their conversations to impress their friends, often interjecting certain Latin phrases *ad nauseam.*

G. Hobby Number 7: Genealogy

The advent of research in the field of genetics and ancestry provides not only an interesting hobby but also the opportunity for cultural and familial enrichment. Most research will require some level of investment in order to procure a membership in one of the various genealogy web-based organizations, but if you are serious about researching your heritage, then it is well worth it. You can even send off a sample of your own saliva for DNA analysis. For most Indoorsman, the results of such prove to be nothing to spit at.

H. Hobby Number 8: Other Possible Indoorsman Hobbies

It would be impossible to exhaustively describe every possible hobby, but other honorable mentions include but are not limited to juggling; yo-yoing; Ping-Pong; leather crafting; model building; Lego construction; painting (the artistic kind, not the home-improvement kind); drawing; origami; listening to music; playing a musical instrument; amateur video production; miniature war gaming; role-playing games; making your own Popsicles in the freezer using orange juice, ice trays, and toothpicks; and rock skipping in the bathtub.

7. OTHER MISCELLANEOUS SITUATIONS

The life of the Indoorsman is riddled with unique and unexpected challenges, which is why it is imperative to internalize not just random facts about handling specific scenarios, but also principles for miscellaneous situations.

On that note, here are some random facts about handling a few specific situations, beginning with how to move quietly through a dark house without waking the other occupants.

A. Three Secrets for Moving Quietly Through a House in the Dark

1. *Heel-first stepping.* When you walk, gently let your heel touch the ground first before slowly laying down the rest of your foot. This method of stepping will keep you well balanced and also keep you from making much noise.

2. *Identify familiar LED lights for reference points.* When you are attempting to navigate an indoor space in extreme darkness, bumping into furniture or doors can cause much noise and wake those who are sleeping. A good trick is to find familiar LED lights from the cable box, the smoke alarm, the microwave, or other subtle electronic displays. These will help you find your bearings even if you cannot see everything in the room in which you are gingerly walking.

3. *Utilize the one-eye-blind trick.* Nothing can cause you to go blind and run into things more than turning on a light in a bathroom (after closing the door) and then reentering a dark room. This is especially true in less familiar indoor spaces such as hotel rooms. Because your eyes will have adjusted to the light, the room you are reentering will seem pitch-black, creating a greater potential for making noise or even injuring yourself. A good trick is to close one eye when you turn on the bathroom light, keeping it closed throughout your short visit. This will keep this eye from adjusting to the light. Then when you reenter the dark room, open this eye and close the other one. The result will be that your one eye will still be acclimated to the darkness, allowing you to navigate the dark room as if you had never left. Be sure to close the other eye, though, as opening both eyes will cause you to become disoriented because one eye will be light adjusted and the other dark adjusted.

B. Loss of Wi-Fi

Losing Wi-Fi service is the modern pestilence of our time. It can strike at any moment, in any weather situation, and without any warning. The following steps may spare you from a complete breakdown in this scenario.

STEPS FOR RESPONDING TO A LOSS OF WI-FI

1. Remember that no matter what you may be feeling right now, life is not meaningless.

2. If you are on a device, try switching to LTE settings. If you don't have a data plan on your device to do so, uh, dude, get a data plan. You did this to yourself.

3. Resist the urge to hold your phone higher or in a different position trying to catch more signal. It's not a walkie-talkie. You're only embarrassing yourself.

4. Unplug your router for 60 seconds and then plug it back in.

5. If that doesn't work, your internet service has probably been interrupted and there is nothing you can do but watch and pray—or drive to your nearest Starbucks and use their Wi-Fi instead.

C. Toilet Paper Outage

No other technological advent on earth better exemplifies the glorious separation between an outdoor existence and an indoor existence than toilet paper. In fact, just for a few seconds, try to imagine what your life would be like without toilet paper. It's not pretty, is it?

STEPS FOR RESPONDING
TO A TOILET PAPER OUTAGE

1. The unfortunate reality is that most people don't discover a TP outage until they are already engaged in the business for which TP is required. Such moments leave you in a compromised position, to say the least. But if you are married, simply yell for your spouse to bring you more TP.

2. If you live alone or are at home alone, you have a tougher row to hoe. You may have to venture outside of the bathroom in an unclean state in search of TP. Proceed with an elevated sense of swiftness and caution. The last thing you want is for someone to enter the house to find you in the middle of your TP search.

3. If after you have awkwardly explored your indoor space only to find that all of your TP reserves have been depleted, then you have officially hit rock bottom, so to speak. Try to find a box of tissues instead.

4. If the search for tissues doesn't work, prepare yourself for pain, but reach for the paper towels.

5. If for some reason your entire world has imploded and there is no TP, no tissues, and no paper towels, if you have small children, try to track down a pack of baby wipes.

6. If all of these options prove fruitless, you may have to take matters into your own hands—*no*, not like that! *Never* like that. Look for copy paper, notebook paper, wax paper, leaves from your fake interior plant, your kid's old homework, or anything else that can help you resolve this most urgent of issues.

7. After the issue is resolved, dispose of all related paraphernalia and wipe down your indoor space as though it were a crime scene (because it sort of is), leaving no evidence of what has occurred recently. In extreme cases, some people have burned their homes to the ground and begun rebuilding their lives afresh atop the rubble of such a recently sordid past.

8. Never speak of this to anyone. (This includes diaries and journals.)

CONNECTING WITH PEOPLE INDOORS

Friendship [indoors] is unnecessary, like philosophy,
like art.... It has no survival value; rather it is one
of those things that gives value to survival.

C.S. LEWIS

The Indoorsman has a reputation of being prone to social isolation, but this is not always a fair assessment. Again, the Indoorsman's life is a complex tapestry that cannot be judged by a singular thread. So as you grow in your level of Indoorsmanship, it will be advantageous to heed the wisdom of others in the area of connection. The following tips may help.

1. YOUR SPOUSE

The indoors is an ideal place to connect with the one whom you love the most. It is literally the shared space of your shared life. You must not let the introverted slant of your Indoorsman angle on life lead you into any obtuse situations with your spouse.

A. Designate Bathrooms

If you have multiple bathrooms, pick one for yourself and stick with it. Nothing can wreck marital bliss quicker than sharing a bathroom—especially a toilet. One's bathroom is the most intimate of indoor spaces, becoming more than just a small room but also a small part of one's heart. Therefore, while it is not advised to have separate bank accounts in one's marriage, it is advised to have separate bathrooms.

B. Make Yours a Double

If you prepare a snack or drink for yourself, make two of each. This wisdom has been around for years, dating back to ancient Indoorsman creeds. There is nothing more divisive than showing up on the couch or to bed with a snack, dessert, or drink only for yourself. Such action often elicits the following response: "Wow. That looks good... Did you make only one?" It is an awkward tale as old as time. So if you will simply make an extra one for your spouse, you will connect with them on a whole new level.

C. Do Not Watch Ahead

Marriage is serious business, and so is Netflix. Being involved together in a dramatic or comedic narrative interwoven into an online or DVRed series is a journey you and your spouse are taking hand in hand—or at least when your hands touch at the bottom of a bag of chips you are sharing in bed. You share the ups and the downs of the butler's life on *Downton Abbey* or Meredith's seventh plane crash on *Grey's Anatomy.* So if one of you is traveling or not at home, the other must never watch ahead by their lonesome. To do so is to disrupt the delicate cohesion shared equally by both members of this marriage. If you want to stay connected indoors, disconnect from shared shows when your spouse is not home.

2. YOUR KIDS

Much of your time as a parent will be spent indoors, so you might as well become acquainted with the best ways to connect with these little humans who share your name and your DNA.

A. Install Master Bedroom Locks

As a parent, you will want to make as many memorable moments with your children as possible. But the real key to quality relationships with your children is enforced moments of separation. This does not mean you should do so in any sort of cruel or negligent way. If they really need you or if the house is burning down, you should obviously make yourself immediately available. However, making sure there is a lock on your master bedroom will keep you the master of your indoor domain, and your children will love you for it—someday.

B. When They Won't Answer, Just Leave the Bathroom Door Unlocked

Every parent reaches a moment when they feel disconnected from their kid. It can feel as if no matter what you say, they simply cannot hear you. The surefire way to reconnect with your kid in these moments is to go to your private bathroom and leave the door unlocked. Scientists are still studying to find the exact cause, but it is an undeniable fact that children will instinctively seek out their parents when they are alone in the bathroom. You can call for them over and over again from the kitchen, and they will never come. But if you will only go into your bathroom and leave the door unlocked, your kids will miraculously find you in less than two minutes—without being called for.

Similarly, if you want your kids to listen to what you're saying, simply lower your voice and begin sharing what seems to be a secret with your spouse or another adult. This will almost magically cause your children to stop screaming, playing with their devices, or otherwise generally ignoring you. They will lean in and attempt to overhear what you are saying. So one can conclude that kids are more prone to *over*hear than to actually hear, hence the effectiveness of such techniques.

3. YOUR DOG

Pets are people too.[1] Regardless, if you have the right kind of pet—namely, a dog (see chapter 8)—you can enjoy memorable moments of indoor entertainment with your dog and perhaps even at his expense.

A. Invest in a Doggie Bed

Much like children, one of the keys to a quality indoor relationship with your pet is establishing effective boundaries. While you may really think you love your dog, the last thing you want is Fido sharing a pillow with you and rolling over in the morning to lick your face with doggie morning breath. You're better than this. Buy a dog bed and teach your dog to use it for sleeping. If you have a small dog, this bed may even fit at the foot of your own bed. But if you do not create some sort of alternative sleeping space, you can expect gradual and unwanted pet encroachment into your own valuable, personal space.

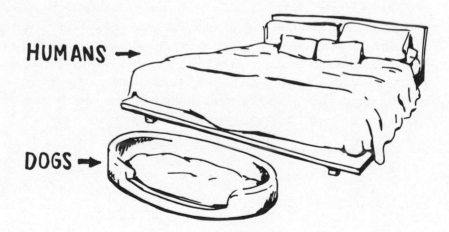

B. Develop an Alter Ego and Accompanying Voice for Your Dog

In the movie *Cast Away*, Tom Hanks is stranded on an island away from the indoors. As expected, the outdoors drives him mad. His only source of comfort is

---

1. This is not true, but it seems to be a common misconception in modern society.

Wilson, a volleyball with a bloody handprint that disturbingly resembles a face. It is his daily conversation with Wilson that keeps Hanks going. Your dog is much the same. Beyond belly rubs and extra treats (and you should consider these for your dog too), you really can't connect with him on a conversational level—until now. If it's good enough for Tom Hanks, it's good enough for the Indoorsman. Develop a voice for your dog, and then talk back and forth with him. This can make for hours of fun, and you may even learn something. You should be mindful not to use this voice when people are around who will either judge or mock you for it—like your visiting pest control specialist or your Outdoorsman brother-in-law at the family Christmas party.

C. Blame Your Dog for Outrageous Things

Once you've established your dog's alter ego, you can really begin to connect with him by blaming him for the outrageous things you know he could never do or even conceive of doing. This technique should be reserved for those moments when your kids or spouse are around, namely, those who know you speak for your dog in his alter ego. At that point, you can blame the dog for eating too much dessert (which you just did), forgetting to turn off the lights (which you forgot to do), and passing gas (which you just did). Placing blame on your dog and then having him defend himself against your accusations in the voice in which you are speaking for him is like a pet version of the movie *Inception*.[2]

4. YOUR FAMILY AND FRIENDS

As much as every Indoorsman cherishes his or her moments of solitude, life in the real world requires a healthy amount of visitation from family and friends. Do not resist these—they are actually necessary for a well-rounded life. The real question is, how often should you engage in these activities? A good rule of thumb is at least once a quarter and certainly not less than this. Regardless of frequency, a few

---

2. This comparison refers to the movie *Inception* starring Leonardo DiCaprio, in which certain people find a way to enter other people's dreams and implant thoughts therein, thus causing the dreamers to feel inclined to enact these seemingly random thoughts after they wake. Such implantation becomes a slippery slope because there are so many levels to the dreams that it becomes easy to forget what is real, as is the case with blaming your dog and then defending him to yourself in the voice you have conjured for him.

tips will help your time of connection with them in your indoor space to move past tolerable and perhaps even into the realm of enjoyable.

A. Set More Than a Starting Time

If you invite family or friends to hang out in your indoor space, you will almost always set an arrival time. But many Novice Indoorsmen fail to also set an informal departure time. Of course, there are some friends and family whose company you will gladly endure over clinking glasses and laughter into the wee hours of the morning. But most visits do not fall into this category, so it is wise to set an anticipated departure time when you set the arrival time. Your text may look something like this: "Hey, guys! Can't wait to hang out tomorrow night. Let's get started at 6:00, but we have to get the baby to bed around 8:30. Kids! Am I right? Ha-ha." These kinds of expectations will make your connection time more effective and enjoyable, as it will be in a more concentrated time frame.

B. Buy a Floor-Cleaning Robot

Much like the reasons to use paper products, at least some of the apprehension of the Indoorsman over the matter of entertaining arises from the amount of time required after the event to return his or her space to a socially acceptable state of cleanliness (or at least some facsimile of the same). This anxiety can bleed over into the actual social event, causing the Indoorsman to walk around and straighten pillows, put down coasters, and cast a stink eye at all the children who are lingering too close to the couch with their drinks. Doing these things in excess while guests are present can make you appear aloof and unengaging—in a bad way. So a great idea is to invest in an automatic floor-cleaning robot. Just the

knowledge that someone else (albeit someone with artificial intelligence) is going to sweep and mop the floor after your guests leave will alleviate much of the angst you are feeling at their persisting presence in your indoor space. Just try to remember not to release your robot to do its work while the guests are still there, as you do not want anyone tripping over it or, even worse, breaking it. Also, consider ascribing a pet name to your robot, such as Edward Bristlehands or Sir Scrubs-a-Lot.

5. CONNECTING IN PUBLIC INDOOR SPACES

The great indoors is not at all confined to *your* indoors, no matter how great it may be. There are many large spaces that also qualify as the indoors, although not all of them require intentional, programmed social interaction. Large arenas and roofed stadiums that hold athletic events, concert halls, malls, restaurants, convention centers, and other large indoor structures generally host many people, but there is not necessarily an expectation that those who are there should connect with one another.

There are, however, other large indoor spaces where this expectation is very real. Such spaces include large work meetings, churches, conferences at which you are registered (often held at large hotels or convention ballrooms), and others. In these moments, you must prepare yourself for what feels like extroverted interaction with other humans. Wisdom says you should not just avoid people outright—again, interaction with people is a healthy part of life—but this interaction should be filtered or even rerouted through some very specific techniques that will allow you to connect and yet maintain the Indoorsman's social prerogatives.

A. Beware the Meet and Greet

Most conferences and church services will intentionally program moments to mingle with the general population in attendance. Yes, this can be terrifying for the Indoorsman, but resist the urge to simply ignore those around you. The best practice is to force yourself to shake hands and interact with one or two people, but after that, your social capacity will most likely be overflowing like a malfunctioning septic tank. To avoid overexposure to more prospective meeters and greeters, you can employ some techniques to neutralize the situation. These include breaking out into a coughing and sneezing fit, slipping out to the bathroom, going to grab a coffee, and for extreme social emergencies, holding your phone to your ear and pretending to be on a very important call.

B. Seek Out Indoorsman Ways to Engage

In situations where social interaction is expected, the Indoorsman can often avoid excessive moments of discomfort by displacing said discomfort with other activities. It is a classic case of choosing to do more than simply avoid the negative by proactively pursuing the positive. Such activities may include drawing on whatever conference notebook or church bulletin that has been passed out to the attendees. Yes, this is an old-school tactic, but it still works, and it seems less socially offensive in the modern age than zoning out on your phone.

You can also get ahead of the discomfort by volunteering at the event to work behind the scenes, perhaps in the lighting, sound, or backstage departments. This is especially effective if you can secure a headset, because people will assume you are in an important programming conversation via your headphones, even if you are listening to nothing but sweet silence. You can also bypass much awkwardness by intentionally recruiting other Indoorsmen from the organization and creating a separate small group with them. You might even consider meeting with them predominantly through Skype from the comfort of your respective indoor domains.

C. Master a Few Elements of Small Talk

In moments when interaction with strangers is unavoidable, despite how violently you have been coughing and sneezing, it will behoove you to have several techniques for making small talk at your disposal. These include but are not limited to the following pointers:

1. *Begin by saying "Hey" instead of "Hello."* Non-Indoorsmen seem to consider it much less formal, although research on the subject continues to grow.

2. *Try to maintain eye contact for 30 seconds at a time.* You will be tempted

to let your eyes wander while the other person is talking, which can make you appear aloof and standoffish. So look them in the eyes and count to 30 in your head, trying not to move your lips, which will make you look crazy to them, defeating the purpose of this tactic in the first place.

3. *If after meeting them, you've already forgotten their name, don't wing it.* Just ask them again. Many a rookie Indoorsman has faltered here by attempting to say someone's name using whatever first letter they can remember. The results can be disastrous. Saying, "It was great to meet you! What was your name again?" is a much better option than saying, "Well, it was nice to meet you, M-m-m-m-armalade?" ("Uh, it's Marla," they will surely reply, but the damage will have been irreversibly done.)

6. CONNECTING WITH THE OUTDOORSMAN USING ACCEPTABLE GIBBERISH

The best way to keep a conversation with an Outdoorsman going in the right direction is to ask questions, but to do so in a way that does not expose your ignorance of the outdoors. Once you get the hang of it, you'll never feel lost in a conversation with an Outdoorsman again. Gibberish-based questions can include:

1. Thingamabobber

Example: "What's that thingamabobber called again?"

2. Dangboy

Example: "Dangboy! You ain't lyin'!"

3. Dat dare

Example: "Dangboy! You ain't lyin' 'bout dat dare thingamabobber!"

4. Ousome

Example: "Dangboy! You ain't lyin' 'bout dat dare thingamabobber bein' ousome!"

5. Gitgo

Example: "Dangboy! You ain't lyin' 'bout dat dare thingamabobber bein' ousome from the gitgo!"

6. Goewoewngit

Example: "Dangboy! You ain't lyin' 'bout dat dare thingamabobber bein' ousome from the gitgo... Ima goewoewngit one fer myself!"

7. OTHER MISCELLANEOUS CONNECTION ISSUES

A. Fist Bumping

As the modern age persists, fist bumping is becoming more and more accept-able as an alternative to handshaking. Its benefits are evident, but none are more sig-

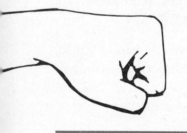

nificant than the fact that by keeping one's hand closed when touching someone else's hand, there is much less risk of passing germs that can cause disease and even death. In a very literal sense, fist bumping is saving lives.

But you should not just jump straight into fist bump-ing without some training.

THREE BASICS OF FIST BUMPING

1. *Don't prematurely "show fist."* Showing your fist is a fairly self-explanatory practice. It refers to creating a fist and coming in for a bump. But your attempt to connect can quickly become awkward if the person to whom you are showing your fist is showing his palm instead. He thinks you are about to shake hands. Besides the social awkwardness, such a mishap can create injuries, especially if you are coming in too hot with your prospective fist bump. The result can be that you just punched a guy. So be careful not to show your fist until you know that the other person will reciprocate.

2. *Avoid the fist punch.* Many overeager Novice Indoorsmen get too excited about a prospective fist bump and accidentally punch the other fist instead. The result is painful for both persons, but generally neither one will display any pain in order to avoid social embarrassment. The best practice is to be mindful of the velocity and strength with which you are attempting to bump. If you are a firm handshaker, then you will probably also be a firm fist bumper. So you'll want to adjust your velocity accordingly to avoid injury or embarrassment.

3. *Avoid post-bump variations.* When the fist bump first hit popular culture, many variations arose. The most popular one was the explosion, which entails pulling back and opening up as if your fist is exploding. For the Avid Indoorsman, the best practice is to keep it to a simple bump unless you are fist bumping younger children, who often laugh at fist bump variations. Otherwise, a simple bump is the safest bet, especially to avoid any undue embarrassment that could arise (similarly to number 1) from attempting some sort of post-bump variation that is not reciprocated by your counterpart.

B. Call Screening

It is appropriate that this topic would be a stopping point for this portion of your Indoorsman training, as it appropriately addresses the dichotomy that exists in the life of the Indoorsman between healthy connection and establishing boundaries for avoiding excessive connection.

The advent of cellular phones and digital communication devices affords individuals the opportunity to connect with others at a moment's notice. But sometimes you will simply want that moment to yourself. This has led to the practice of call screening, which means that you see who is calling you, but you decline their call even though you technically could talk. It simply means that you don't want to talk to them.

This has become a very offensive action in certain social circles, so you would be wise to become familiar with some philosophical insights for screening calls.

THREE INSIGHTS ABOUT SCREENING CALLS

1. *Most calls are not obligations.*

   When your phone begins to ring (or vibrate) and you see who is calling you, you have a decision to make. No matter how upset anyone may become, that decision is yours and no one can take it away from you. Embrace your freedom.

   Obviously, if it is your spouse, your mother, or your children calling, you should always answer. Otherwise, just because the world has the *ability* to talk to you on your phone 24 hours each day does not mean they have the *right* to talk to you 24 hours a day. Take back your life. Screen a call every once in a while with no shame.

2. *All incoming calls are not created equal.*

   Because equality does not exist regarding all incoming calls, they should not have equal access to your time and energy. When your phone rings, you have to mentally process a few questions. Will talking to this person cause you immediate emotional distress? Are they one of those people with whom you've never had a conversation that lasted less than 40 minutes? Do you need time to prepare yourself emotionally for this call or this person? Will you suffer any immediate family friction for not answering?

3. *Choose wisely.*

After you have processed these questions, embrace the freedom to choose whether to answer or decline. You may even consider declining the call and sending an immediate text. This could salvage your time by avoiding a long conversation and yet allow the information from the call to be still successfully communicated.

But if you do choose to answer, the person who calls you is earning the right to make your answer list in the future. For example, if they snarkily say, "Wow! You answered your phone this time," you may choose to respond with something like, "Well, I kind of regret that I did now." Again, those who desire your time on the phone will quickly begin to understand that talking to an Avid Indoorsman on the phone is a privilege, not a right.

C. When You Must Go Outdoors

Obviously, there are times when you will have to go outdoors due to your relationships with the people you love and for whom you care. Yes, you can minimize these occurrences by ordering online, engaging in modern food delivery methods, consolidating your errands to decrease the number of trips you have to make, and asking your friends for a lot of favors, but even with these techniques, there will be unavoidable moments when you must go outdoors because your life situation demands it or because you have been invited out by someone else. Inescapable scenarios include but are not limited to the following.

SIX MOST LIKELY INESCAPABLE
OUTDOOR SCENARIOS

1. An outdoor family wedding

2. Taking a family member or friend for a visit to the doctor or hospital

3. A graveside funeral service

4. Your kid's football, soccer, baseball, softball, or lacrosse game (Again, consider helping your kids to choose indoor sports, such as swimming, volleyball, basketball, curling, and chess.)

5. A close friend's birthday celebration in which he or she wants to play golf, go camping, or engage in some other outdoor activity

6. Falling out of a helicopter and waking up to find yourself lost in a dense forest

While there are techniques to remember if you ever find yourself in these or any other outdoor situations, you should familiarize yourself with every conceivable excuse for getting out of such scenarios.

TWELVE BEST EXCUSES FOR
AVOIDING THE OUTDOORS

1. "My goldfish really needs my attention right now."

2. "My allergies are flaring up." (Follow that with a convincing sneeze.)

3. "I just started shampooing my rug, and…well, you know."

4. "If I go outside, I come down with polymorphous light eruption— PMLE. It's an allergy to the sun. I know. Crazy, right?"

5. "I have a suspicious rash." (Which is unrelated to your PMLE.)

6. "I need to plan my wardrobe for the week."

7. "I need to call my mom."

8. "I'm working to disprove gravity, and it's really getting me down."

9. "I'm thinking about taking up knitting, and tonight I'm scrapbooking a chart of pros and cons."

10. "I need to design a flannelgraph layout for Sunday school. So, yeah, I'm staring down another all-nighter."

11. "I pulled that big muscle in my baby toe again."

12. "I'm going to my cousin's best friend's baby's first birthday."

PUTTING IT ALL TOGETHER

Back before the internet (when dinosaurs roamed the earth), there was such a thing as an encyclopedia. No, it was not a one-eyed, hurricane-like monster from ancient Greek mythology, although that could work well in any one of the 27 superhero movies that are released every year.[1] Rather, it was an exhaustive collection of alphabetized definitions and explanations about everything under the sun (as well as many things out in space, that is, "over" the sun). This information was contained in many large leather-bound volumes and filled entire bookcases in smart people's libraries and offices.[2] Encyclopedias were things of beauty. Pristine and meticulous resources to aid the young and the aged alike in the universal quest for knowledge about everything from aardvarks to xylophones and everything in between (and after as well[3]).

But much like whatever catastrophic event annihilated the dinosaurs, the internet crashed onto the printed world and sent it rolling like a flaming eight ball into some proverbial global corner pocket.[4] In terms of their printed popularity, it was "game over" for encyclopedias. Even so, the information they once were intended to contain seemed to simultaneously blow up as well, to the extent that there was

---

1. They have to run out of villain concepts soon, right?

2. Really intelligent people have been known to call their home library or office a study.

3. Everything in between and after, because the encyclopedia would have taught you that xylophone begins with an x and not a z.

4. Too many metaphors? I can never tell.

no longer enough shelf space in one's study to house leather-bound beauties containing the vast array of knowledge so speedily coming to light.

Obviously, as an official and authoritative voice on the subject of Indoorsmanship, the author of this work could not be more grateful for the advent of the internet and its accompanying technological advances. The point here is about the exponential growth of information.

Such is also the case for the subject of Indoorsmanship. This book is but an inaugural volume 1 (if you will) in a field that continues to expand at an immeasurable pace. To that end, do not consider the information you have gleaned from these few pages to be a complete picture. It is more like a single frozen frame in a motion picture reel. A snapshot, not the whole movie.

Hopefully, these pages have whetted your appetite or at least caused you to stop, think, and maybe even smile a bit. Perhaps you will remember how to avoid outdoor dangers such as Bigfoot, the Loch Ness Monster, and dirt. Maybe you will heed the wisdom offered in these pages and avoid FOMA (fear of miscellaneous assembly) when you gather with your family at the next Christmas party. Perhaps you will find new moments of introverted relaxation when you adopt Indoorsman showering techniques or avoid social embarrassment when you choose to lose your Eager Fuzzbucket beard in favor of the Patient Apprentice.

Regardless, the highest hopes for you are that you will not only continue to apply these principles to your life but also add to them as if you were penning new volumes in your own set of encyclopedias. You must put it all together for a holistic Indoorsman life.

One example might be putting together the information on increasing your lifespan by standing up longer each day (chapter 7) with the research-based theory of sleep superfluity (chapter 6), which states that sleeping 15 hours each day will guarantee you will survive 115 years. Put them together and what have you got? Bippity, boppity, *spoon*. Spooning here meaning sleeping closely while living longer with your spouse by developing a technique to sleep standing up for 15 hours a day so that you can reach early Old Testament lifespans. Strap yourself and your loved ones into your Methuselah memory foam mattress and get to living—really living!

Regardless of how you do it, be creative, be exhaustive, and put it all together as you enjoy the Indoorsman life. And remember, don't just be safe *out there*. Be safe *in here*.

ACKNOWLEDGMENTS

Obviously, it would be impossible for me to mention everyone in my life who has encouraged, supported, or endured me on my writing journey. Nevertheless, it's my great honor to at least mention a few. Just know that there are many more, and I am thankful for you all.

I'm forever grateful to Robert Wolgemuth, my incomparable literary agent. Half a decade ago you took a chance on me as a writer, but you have always graciously encouraged me in so much more than just this craft. Austin Wilson, my other incredible agent, you have truly stayed in the trenches with me through every crazy project, pitch, and idea—and beyond that, you have become a dear friend for whom I am so grateful.

Kyle Hatfield, Kim Moore, Heather Green, and the rest of the incredible team at Harvest House, you literally made this book happen. Thank you for your hilarious concept, your clever ideas, and your unyielding kindness from start to finish. You guys truly are the best.

From my dear friend Reggie Dabbs, who first asked me to write a book *with* you, to Tim Hawkins, Todd Wagner, Dave and Ann Wilson, and all the others who have inconceivably done the same, I am eternally grateful to each of you for the humbling honor of stewarding your voices and stories. A thousand libraries could not contain what I have learned from you.

To all my friends, past and present, from the Church at Pleasant Grove—thank you for always supporting me, encouraging me, and being willing to live authentic life with me. And to the entire staff who diligently and faithfully works alongside me each and every day, I am so grateful to fail, succeed, grow, and lead with such amazing champions and friends.

John Carey, who never ceases to encourage me in every endeavor of my life, I am always grateful for you. And Andrew Wharton…where do I begin? You are a constant friend, compatriot, and guiding force in my story. I literally would not be writing without your courage, honesty, and friendship.

Jonnie Wethington (Jonnie W., to the layperson), you have been like a brother to me for more than 20 years. Most of what I think of as funny came from hanging out with you…so if this book tanks, we both know whom to blame. Love you, bro.

My family, the Canadas—I am overwhelmed by your love and support. I hope you genuinely chuckle at my lighthearted satire directed toward the outdoorsman…and I really do hope I will still get a Christmas present this year. My family, the Drivers—I am forever enriched by each of you in unforgettable ways. If Dad's family motto still rings true, I am forever grateful to be working on the impossible, which takes a little longer than the mere difficult, with all of you.

My dearest Sadie, who makes me laugh out loud every day, you truly are my favorite, and I couldn't be more grateful to be the daddy of such a creative, thoughtful, generous, brilliant, and beautiful daughter.

And finally, Laura, the one who is constantly at my side—there are no words to express the depths of my love and gratitude for the life we blissfully enjoy together every day, even when circumstances are not so blissful. But as you already know, I will spend the rest of our lives searching for more words anyway…and in the most verbose way possible. I guess you can say that my love for you knows no word count.

ABOUT THE AUTHOR

John Driver may be strange, but he is no stranger to the indoors. Originally born inside a hospital, he still sleeps in a bedroom and usually takes showers in a bathroom.

A mediocre wordsmith with a dull sense of wit coupled with keenly senseless verbosity, he has been on a lifelong mission to equip the Indoorsmen and Indoorswomen of the world as well as those who dream of joining their ranks with every seemingly useless tool and fact imaginable. For years, millions of Indoorsmen have languished in the shadows of shame and obscurity. But now, through the work John is selfishly pursuing to the detriment of maintaining a steady income, they can languish in the light instead.

John lives with his wife, Laura, and their daughter, Sadie, near Nashville, Tennessee, where, surprisingly, he works at actual indoor jobs as a writer, podcaster, and minister.

More information is available at: www.johndriver.com.

To learn more about Harvest House books and
to read sample chapters, visit our website:

www.harvesthousepublishers.com

HARVEST HOUSE PUBLISHERS
EUGENE, OREGON